STEVEN MANN

Using PowerShell with SharePoint 2013

Using PowerShell with SharePoint 2013

Trademarks

Warning and Disclaimer

Table of Contents

Appendixes

Getting Started

CHAPTER 1

SharePoint 2013 Management Shell Overview

This chapter is a brief overview of the PowerShell and SharePoint 2013 Management Shell console applications. It provides foundational information on the logistics behind running scripts for SharePoint 2013.

Starting PowerShell

On every Windows Server running Windows Server 2008 or higher, PowerShell is installed and may be used for administration purposes. By default, the PowerShell application appears in the Windows taskbar. Right-clicking the application button displays available menu options as shown in Figure 1.1.

Figure 1.1 The PowerShell application button provides a menu of options

Clicking on the Import System Modules, launches PowerShell and loads all modules from all services and server applications running

4

on the current server. This is useful when scripting out code for more than one set of services.

Clicking the Windows PowerShell ISE, launches a development environment where you may create, execute, and debug PowerShell scripts.

Selecting the Windows PowerShell menu item launches PowerShell without loading any modules. You may select the Run As Administrator menu item to launch PowerShell with administrative privileges.

Loading the SharePoint Module

Launching PowerShell on the server opens a blue console application window. Without importing any modules, this instance does not know how to execute any SharePoint commands. To make this PowerShell instance aware of SharePoint, you must add the SharePoint PowerShell snap-in using the following command (as shown in Figure 1.2):

```
Add-PsSnapIn Microsoft.SharePoint.PowerShell
```

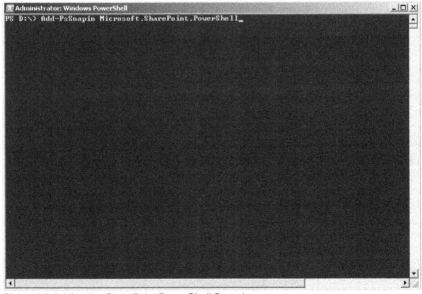

Figure 1.2 Adding the SharePoint PowerShell Snap-In

5

Using the SharePoint 2013 Management Shell

The SharePoint 2013 Management Shell is a variation of PowerShell geared towards the administration and management of SharePoint. Once SharePoint is installed on the server, the management console is available from the Start menu as shown in Figure 1.3.

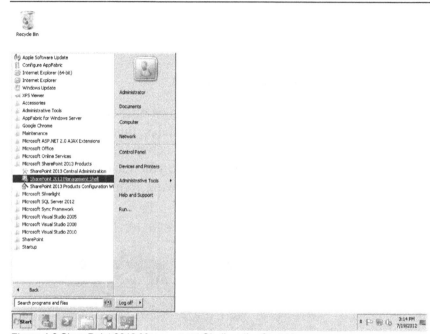

Figure 1.3 SharePoint 2013 Management Shell on the Start Menu

Selecting the SharePoint 2013 Management Shell launches the management console as shown in Figure 1.4.

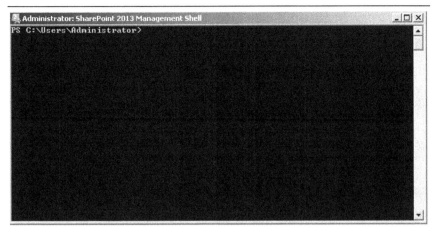

Figure 1.4 SharePoint 2013 Management Shell Console Window

The management console window knows about SharePoint commands as well as general PowerShell commands and may be used to execute command lines or scripts. Some PowerShell basics are outlined in Chapter 2.

Intentionally BLANK

Basic Definitions and Concepts

This chapter explains about some of the PowerShell basics to acquire a general understanding. The sections in this chapter help form a foundation for the tasks within this book.

Defining Cmdlets

PowerShell commands are called cmdlets. These are structured by a verb and noun concatenation in the form of verb-noun. So in the cmdlet "Get-Help", Get is the verb and Help is the noun. (Use the Get-Help cmdlet to view helpful information in working with cmdlets.)

Viewing Verbs

If you know the noun but are unsure of the possible verbs available, you can enter the noun with a "-?" to display the available verb-noun combinations. This may also provide additional nouns that are similar to the one you provided. For example, "SPSite -?" not only displays the available verbs for the SPSite noun but also for SPSiteAdministration, SPSiteSubscription, and other cmdlets available beginning with SPSite.

Using Parameters

Most cmdlets need values to perform the desired actions. These values are provided to the cmdlet using parameters in the following form:

-parametername <value>

Using Switch Parameters

A switch parameter is a parameter used with a cmdlet that does not take a value (or are Boolean in nature and can be set to a "false" setting). The fact that the switch parameter is present "switches" that option on ("true" setting) when executing the cmdlet.

Most of the time switch parameters are optional but in some cases you may need to provide one switch or another. This is dependent on the cmdlet being executed.

Viewing Parameters for a Cmdlet

Entering the cmdlet in the console with "-?" as a parameter, displays information about that cmdlet along with the available parameters. An example is shown in Listing 2.1.

LISTING 2.1 **Getting Information about a Cmdlet**

```
Get-SPSite -?
```

Some cmdlets have different variations of parameters. These variations will also be displayed within the information provided by the "-?" parameter as shown in Figure 2.1.

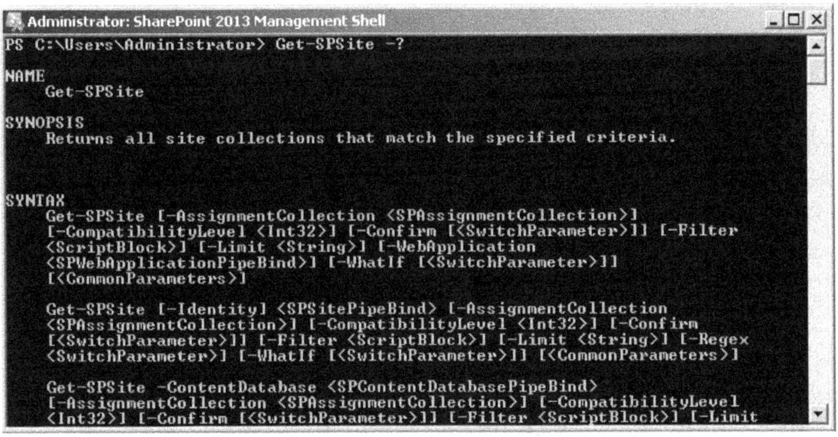

Figure 2.1 Using "-?" with a cmdlet provides parameter and syntax information

11

Using the F3 Function Key

Pressing the F3 function key in the console window displays the last executed statement on the current prompt line. Using the up and down arrows will page through the other previous statements. This is useful for repeating or correcting previous command entries. Use the left and right arrow keys to place the cursor within the command text for corrections.

Using the F7 Function Key

Pressing the F7 function key displays a menu of previously executed commands as shown in Figure 2.2.

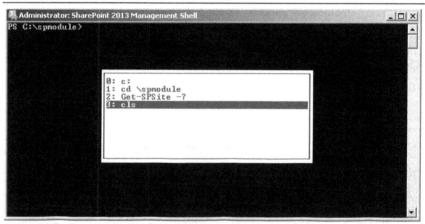

Figure 2.2 Pressing the F7 Function Key Presents the History Menu

Use the arrow keys to change the selection in the menu. Pressing Enter will execute the command selected. Pressing F9 on the menu allows you to enter the command number you wish to re-execute but only places it on the line (does not execute it automatically).

12

Using Console Commands

There are console commands that may be used in any console window including PowerShell and the SharePoint Management shell. These commands provide directory navigation, file handling, and screen handling.

Several common console commands are as follows:

cd: Change directory

cls: Clear the console screen

dir : Display listing of current directory (folder)

type: Used with a text-based file name. This will display the contents of a text file.

Setting the Path Environment Variable

You may add the local folder's path to the PSModule environment variable by entering the following command in the PowerShell command prompt (substituting <folder path> with the local directory path) as shown in Listing 2.2.

LISTING 2.2 **Adding a Folder Path to the PSModulePath**

```
$env:PSModulePath = $env:PSModulePath + ";c:\<folder
path>"
```

Running Unsigned Scripts

In order to be allowed to run unsigned scripts you must change the execution policy:

```
Set-ExecutionPolicy remotesigned
```

You will be prompted with a confirmation. Enter "Y" and press enter (or just press enter since "Y" is the default).

In some cases you may need to set the policy to Unrestricted:

```
Set-ExecutionPolicy unrestricted
```

Disabling the Confirmation Prompt

When running some cmdlets described in this book, you may receive a confirmation message. If you use these cmdlets in scripts, the script will not run straight through without prompting for the confirmation.

The cmdlets that have a –Confirm optional parameter can be called in unattended mode by passing in –Confirm:$false to the cmdlet as shown in Listing 2.3

LISTING 2.3 **Suppressing the Confirmation Prompt Example**

```
Remove-item *.png –Confirm:$false
```

Generating Inline Credentials

Various cmdlets discussed in this book require SharePoint and/or SQL Server account credentials for proper authentication when performing the desired operations. The examples will include using "(Get-Credential)" as the parameter value which prompts the user for credentials.

When running these cmdlets in scripts, the prompting for credentials pauses the execution. If you need the script to run straight through, instead of using Get-Credential, you may generate a new PSCredential object inline as shown in Listing 2.4.

LISTING 2.4 **Generating Inline Credentials Example**

```
(New-Object System.Management.Automation.PSCredential
"domain\user", (ConvertTo-SecureString "password"
-AsPlainText -Force))
```

Therefore, simply substitute (Get-Credential) for the text shown in Listing 2.4 with the proper username and password when using a cmdlet with authentication requirements.

Referencing an Assembly

You may reference an assembly in your PowerShell script and then use any objects available by assigning them to a variable. Any methods or properties can then be used within your script. There is no intellisense so you need to know the object model beforehand. Listing 2.5 demonstrates an example assembly reference and usage.

LISTING 2.5 **Referencing and Using a SharePoint Assembly**

```
[Void][System.Reflection.Assembly]::LoadWithPartialNa
me("Microsoft.SharePoint")
[Void][System.Reflection.Assembly]::LoadWithPartialNa
me("Microsoft.SharePoint.Administration")

$spFarm =
[Microsoft.SharePoint.Administration.SPFarm]::Local
$spFarmSolutions = $spFarm.Solutions
```

PART II

Server Management

Intentionally BLANK

CHAPTER 3

SharePoint 2013 Configuration

Configuring a New SharePoint 2013 Farm

The New-SharePointFarm cmdlet allows you to configure a new SharePoint farm on the server. The syntax is as follows:

New-SharePointFarm -databaseserver <server name>

-databaseaccessaccount (Get-Credential <domain\account>)

-farmname <name of new farm>

-passphrase (ConvertTo-SecureString -asplaintext -force -string "Enter a farm pass phrase here")

This command requires credentials for the database server. Therefore, the Get-Credential PowerShell command is used in conjunction with New-SharePointFarm. After you enter the command, PowerShell will prompt for the password of the database access account entered, as shown in Figure 3.1.

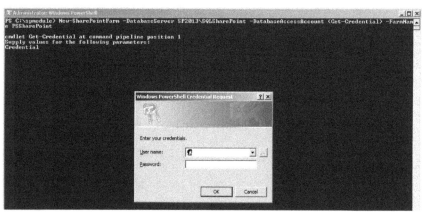

FIGURE 3.1
Using Get-Credential prompts for the corresponding password.

Once the credentials have been entered, the new farm will be configured using the database server entered. You may use inline credentials instead such that you are not prompted (see Chapter 2 for details). This essentially creates the SharePoint_Config database and prepares the farm for use.

The farm passphrase is a password that is used when you are adding new servers to the farm or making farm configuration changes. It needs to be entered into the cmdlet as a secure string; therefore, the ConvertTo-SecureString cmdlet is also used in conjunction with New_SharePointFarm.

Joining a Server to the SharePoint 2013 Farm

The previous cmdlet (New-SharePointFarm) created the database and configured the SharePoint farm. You cannot run this again on the other servers. Instead, you need to join the servers to the farm using the Join-SharePointFarm cmdlet:

Join-SharePointFarm –databaseserver <database server name>

-configurationdatabasename <config database>

-passphrase (ConvertTo-SecureString -asplaintext -force -string

"<farm pass phrase>")

The farm passphrase used with the Join-SharePointFarm cmdlet should be the same passphrase used when you are creating the new SharePoint farm.

Creating a New Web Application

To create a new web application, use the New-SPWebApplication cmdlet as follows:

New-SPWebApplication –applicationpool <name of new application pool>

-name <name of new web app>

-applicationpoolaccount <service account to be used for the

application pool> -port <desired port number>

A sample command-line entry for creating the main SharePoint web application is shown in Listing 3.5.

LISTING 3.5 **Creating a New Web Application**

New-SPWebApplication –applicationpool SharePoint-80

-name SharePoint-80 -applicationpoolaccount SP\AppPoolAccount -port 80

This process may take a few minutes. When it's completed, the display name and the URL of the new web application are presented in the console.

Creating a New Site Collection

To add a new site collection, use the New-SPSite cmdlet, as follows:

New-SPSite –url <full url of new site collection>

-name <name of new site collection>

-owneralias <site collection administrator>

-template <site collection template to use>

A sample command-line entry for creating the root site collection using the Team Site template is shown in Listing 3.6.

LISTING 3.6 **Creating the Root Top-level Site Collection**

```
New-SPSite –url http://sp2013/
        -name Home
        -owneralias SP\SiteAdmin
        -template STS#0
```

The site template names can be found using Get-SPWebTemplates. If no template is provided, the site collection will still be created. In this case, once the site is accessed via the browser, SharePoint will prompt for a site collection template to be selected.

Creating a New Subsite

To create a new subsite, use the New-SPWeb cmdlet as follows:

New-SPWeb –url <full url of new site> -name <name of new site> -template <site template to use>

A few switch parameters are available for the New-SPWeb cmdlet:

- AddToTopNav
- UniquePermissions
- UseParentTopNav

The AddToTopNav switch parameter places the new site within the top navigation of the site collection. Using the Use-ParentTopNav switch parameter replicates the top nav of the site collection onto the new subsite. Creating a site with UniquePer-missions forces the site to not inherit permissions from the site collection and only grants the System Account Full Control access.

A sample command-line entry for creating a subsite using the Team Site template is shown in Listing 3.7.

LISTING 3.7 **Creating a Subsite in the Root Site Collection**

```
New-SPWeb
        -url http://sp2013/PSSubSite
        -name "PS Sub Site"
        -template STS#0
        -AddToTopNav
        -UniquePermissions
        -UseParentTopNav
```

The site template names can be found using Get-SPWebTemplates. If no template is provided, the site will still be created. In this case, once the site is accessed via the browser, SharePoint will prompt for a site template to be selected.

Using both AddToTopNav and UseParentTopNav ensures the new site always appears in the top navigation, as shown in Figure 3.2.

FIGURE 3.2
Using the switch parameters places the subsite in the top nav.

INTENTIONALLY BLANK

CHAPTER 4

SharePoint 2013 Farm Management

This chapter outlines the SharePoint PowerShell commands that are used to manage general operations within your SharePoint farm. Whereas some operations are specific to the farm level, others are overall farm administration cmdlets that could not be categorized into a separate chapter.

Reviewing Your SharePoint 2013 Farm Configuration Values

Several configuration settings are available using SPFarmConfig. Execute the Get-SPFarmConfig without any parameters, as shown in Listing 4.1, to display the current values. Some sample output is shown in Figure 4.1.

LISTING 4.1 **Displaying All Farm Configuration Values**

```
Get-SPFarmConfig
```

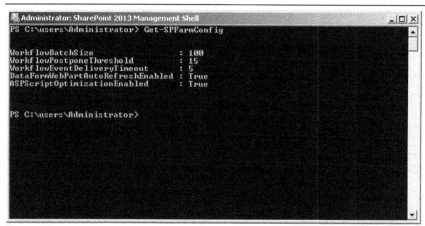

Figure 4.1

Get-SPFarmConfig displays the current farm configuration values.

Setting Your SharePoint 2013 Farm Configuration Values

The values shown in the previous section may be modified using the Set-SPFarmConfig cmdlet with the associated parameter of each value. The parameters for these configuration values are as follows:

- ASPScriptOptimizationEnabled
- DataFormWebPartAutoRefreshEnabled
- WorkflowBatchSize
- WorkflowEventDeliveryTimeout
- WorkflowPostponeThreshold

The ASPScriptOptimizationEnabled parameter is a boolean parameter that determines whether ASP scripting is allowed to be optimized by IIS.

The DataFormWebPartAutoRefreshEnabled parameter is a boolean parameter that determines whether the data form web parts on the SharePoint web pages are allowed to automatically refresh using the asynchronous Ajax settings. If this value is set to false, the data form web parts will not automatically refresh regardless of the web part Ajax settings.

The WorkflowBatchSize value defaults to 100 and determines the amount of events that may be processed for a single workflow instance. The value must be greater than 0 but can be as large as the maximum integer value.

The WorkflowEventDeliveryTimeout parameter specifies the number of minutes that a workflow can run before it times out. The default value is 5 minutes but can be any positive integer. If the workflow times out, it is placed back into the queue to attempt execution again.

The WorkflowPostponeThreshold parameter determines how many workflows may operate at the same time. The default is 15 workflows but can be any integer value. If the amount of workflows that need to run exceed this amount, the excess workflows are placed in the queue and must wait for the running workflows to finish.

The parameter names are exactly the same as the output from Get-SPFarmConfig. A sample command line for setting these values is shown in Listing 4.2.

LISTING 4.2 **Setting the Farm Configuration Values**

```
Set-SPFarmConfig
     -ASPScriptOptimizationEnabled:$true
     -DataFormWebPartAutoRefreshEnabled:$false
     -WorkflowBatchSize 50
     -WorkflowEventDeliveryTimeout 15
     -WorkflowPostponeThreshold 5
```

Run the Get-SPFarmConfig cmdlet to verify your changes.

Refreshing Installed SharePoint 2013 Products

Using the InstalledProductsRefresh switch parameter with the Set-SPFarmConfig cmdlet refreshes the current server's license state with the products installed on the SharePoint farm. A sample command line is shown in Listing 4.3.

LISTING 4.3 **Refreshing the Installed Products**

```
Set-SPFarmConfig -InstalledProductsRefresh
```

Changing the HTTP Port of Central Admin

The Set-SPCentralAdministration cmdlet is solely used to change the port number configured for the Central Administration web application. Provide a valid port number, as shown in Listing 4.4.

LISTING 4.4 **Changing the Port of Central Admin**

```
Set-SPCentralAdministration -Port 12345
```

Changing the SharePoint Farm Passphrase

The Set-SPPassPhrase cmdlet is solely used to change the Share-Point farm passphrase. This passphrase was initially entered during the installation of the SharePoint farm. Provide a secure string value with the PassPhrase parameter, as shown in Listing 4.5.

LISTING 4.5 **Changing the Farm Pass Phrase**

```
Set-SPPassPhrase -PassPhrase
(ConvertTo-SecureString -asplaintext -force -string
"SharePointPassPhrase")
```

For scripting purposes, if you do not wish to be prompted to confirm the passphrase entry, include the ConfirmPassPhrase parameter and switch the general confirmation off, as shown in Listing 4.6.

LISTING 4.6 **Changing the Farm Passphrase Without Prompts**

```
Set-SPPassPhrase
-PassPhrase
     (ConvertTo-SecureString -asplaintext
     -force -string "SharePointPassPhrase")
-ConfirmPassPhrase
     (ConvertTo-SecureString -asplaintext -force -
     string "SharePointPassPhrase")
-Confirm:$false
```

The default operation performs the passphrase modification for the entire farm. If you run into issues, use the LocalServerOnly switch parameter to only perform the modification on the current server. Continue on each server in the farm to pinpoint the problem.

Retrieving the SharePoint 2013 System Accounts

Issuing the Get-SPProcessAccount cmdlet without any parameters displays all system and managed accounts on the SharePoint farm, as shown in Figure 4.2.

Figure 4.2

Get-SPProcessAccount displays all SharePoint system and managed accounts.

32

Several mutually exclusive switch parameters may be used to retrieve a specific system account. The switch parameters are LocalSystem, LocalService, and NetworkService. Use these separately, as shown in Listing 4.7.

LISTING 4.7 **Retrieving Individual System Accounts**

```
Get-SPProcessAccount -LocalSystem
Get-SPProcessAccount -LocalService
Get-SPProcessAccount -NetworkService
```

Retrieving the SharePoint 2013 Managed Accounts

Issuing the Get-SPManagedAccount cmdlet without any parameters displays all managed accounts on the SharePoint farm. To retrieve a specific managed account, you may use the account name, as shown in Listing 4.8.

LISTING 4.8 **Retrieving a Specific Managed Account**

```
Get-SPManagedAccount "SP\SPAdminManagedAccount"
```

Renaming a SharePoint 2013 Site Template

The Set-SPWebTemplate cmdlet is used to update the name and/or description of an installed site template within your SharePoint farm. You need the identity of the site template to update. A sample command line is shown in Listing 4.9.

LISTING 4.9 **Updating the Name and Description of a Site Template**

```
Set-SPWebTemplate -Identity "CUSTOMTEMPLATE#1" -Name
"Custom Site Template" -Description "Custom Template"
```

You may only modify custom site templates. Attempting to modify a system-based site template results in an error.

Renaming a Server on the SharePoint 2013 Farm

The Rename-SPServer cmdlet may be used to rename a server in the farm. This only renames the server from a SharePoint standpoint and does not actually rename the physical server. Use the current name as the Identity parameter and the new name for the Name parameter, as shown in Listing 4.10.

LISTING 4.10 **Renaming a Server on the SharePoint 2013 Farm**

```
Rename-SPServer -Identity "CurrentServerName" -Name
"RevisedServerName"
```

If the rename procedure does not complete successfully, the server being renamed may no longer function as a SharePoint 2013 server. Running the SharePoint 2013 Products Configuration Wizard may resolve any issues; however, there is the potential of configuration database corruption forcing you to rebuild the SharePoint farm.

Displaying the Configured SharePoint 2013 Managed Paths

Issuing the Get-SPManagedPath cmdlet with the WebApplication parameter (as shown in Listing 4.11) displays all configured managed paths on the SharePoint farm, as shown in Figure 4.3.

LISTING 4.11 **Retrieving Configured Managed Paths**

```
Get-SPManagedPath -WebApplication "SharePoint Root
Web App"
```

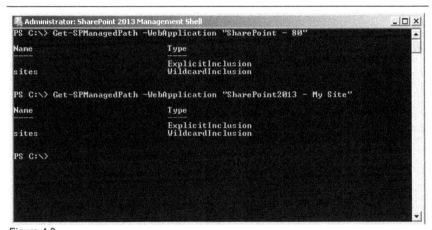

Figure 4.3

Get-SPManagedPath displays all configured managed paths.

Creating a New SharePoint 2013 Managed Path

Using the New-SPManagedPath cmdlet allows you to create a new managed path on the specified web application, as shown in Listing 4.12.

LISTING 4.12 **Creating a New SharePoint 2013 Managed Path**

```
New-SPManagedPath -WebApplication "SharePoint Root
Web App" -RelativeURL "/teamsites/"
```

The forward slashes (/) in the name of the managed path are optional but do provide a visual queue (similar to manually creating a managed path through Central Administration).

By default, the managed path is created as a wildcard inclusion type. You may use the Explicit switch parameter to generate the managed path as an explicit inclusion type, as shown in Listing 4.13.

LISTING 4.13 **Creating a New SharePoint 2013 Managed Path with Explicit Inclusion**

```
New-SPManagedPath -WebApplication "SharePoint Root
Web App" -RelativeURL
"/teamsites/" -Explicit
```

You may also create a managed path using the HostHeader parameter instead of the WebApplication parameter.

Removing a SharePoint 2013 Managed Path

Using the Remove-SPManagedPath cmdlet allows you to remove a managed path from the specified web application, as shown in Listing 4.14.

LISTING 4.14 **Removing a Managed Path**

```
Remove-SPManagedPath -Identity "teamsites"

-WebApplication "SharePoint Root Web App"
```

The Identity parameter is simply the name of the relative URL that was used to generate the managed path, which becomes the name of the managed path. Use the Get-SPManagedPath cmdlet to review the names.

You may also remove a managed path using the HostHeader parameter instead of the WebApplication parameter.

Merging SharePoint 2013 Log Files

The Merge-SPLogFile cmdlet is a wonderful process that will consolidate the logs from all servers in the farm into one log file. This makes it easier to trace and find issues. A sample command line is shown in Listing 4.15.

LISTING 4.15 **Merging Log Files**

```
Merge-SPLogFile -Path E:\Logs\MergedLog.log -
StartTime "8/29/2013" -Overwrite
```

The Path parameter is the path and filename of the log file you wish to create. If it already exists, the cmdlet will fail unless you include the Overwrite switch parameter. You should use the Start-Time parameter (and/or the EndTime parameter) to specify the range of the log entries that should be gathered and merged.

Several other parameters can help you narrow down the log search:

- Area
- Category
- ContextFilter
- Correlation
- Level
- EventID
- Message
- Process
- ThreadID

Closing the Current Log File

The New-SPLogFile cmdlet will stop the current log file and start logging to a new one. This is helpful if you are tracing an issue and do not need more entries in the log file or do not want any issues with the log file being in use. Simply issue the New-SPLogFile cmdlet without any parameters on the server you want to start a new log file, as shown in Listing 4.16.

LISTING 4.16 **Create and Start a New Log File**

```
New-SPLogFile
```

Reviewing SharePoint Designer 2013 Settings

The Get-SPDesignerSettings cmdlet allows you to review the current SharePoint Designer 2013 settings for a specified web application. Running this cmdlet with the WebApplication parameter, as shown in Listing 4.17, displays the current settings, as shown in Figure 4.4.

LISTING 4.17 **Reviewing the SharePoint Designer Settings**

```
Get-SPDesignerSettings -WebApplication "SharePoint
Root Web App"
```

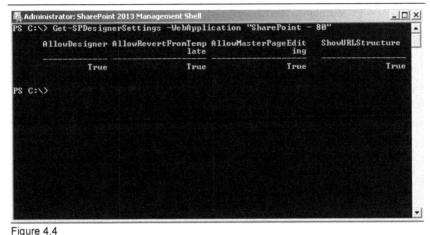

Figure 4.4

Get-SPDesignerSettings displays the SharePoint Designer settings.

Configure SharePoint Designer Settings

The Set-SPDesignerSettings cmdlet allows you to modify the
SharePoint Designer settings for a specific web application. Each
setting, listed here, is a Boolean parameter:

- AllowDesigner
- AllowMasterPageEditing
- AllowRevertFromTemplate
- ShowURLStructure

A sample modification command line is shown in Listing 4.18.

LISTING 4.18 **Modifying the SharePoint Designer Settings**

```
Set-SPDesignerSettings

-WebApplication "SharePoint Root Web App"

-AllowDesigner:$false

-AllowMasterPageEditing:$false

-AllowRevertFromTemplate:$true

-ShowURLStructure:$false
```

The AllowDesigner parameter determines whether the sites in the web application can be modified with SharePoint Designer 2013. The user performing the action must have the proper permissions to modify the site. The default value is True.

The AllowMasterPageEditing parameter determines whether the master pages and page layouts in the sites of the web application can be modified with SharePoint Designer 2013 by site administrators or users with the appropriate permissions. The default value is True.

The AllowRevertFromTemplate parameter specifies whether site pages can be detached from the site definition using SharePoint Designer. The default value is True.

The ShowURLStructure parameter specifies whether the URL structure of the web application may be modified in SharePoint Designer. The default value is True.

Reviewing SharePoint Workflow Configuration Settings

The Get-SPWorkflowConfig cmdlet allows you to review the current workflow configuration settings for a specified web application or site collection. Running this cmdlet with the WebApplication parameter is shown in Listing 4.19. The site collection command line is shown in Listing 4.20. Sample results of both command lines are shown in Figure 4.5.

LISTING 4.19 **Reviewing the Workflow Configuration for a Web Application**

```
Get-SPWorkflowConfig -WebApplication "SharePoint Root
Web App"
```

LISTING 4.20 **Reviewing the Workflow Configuration for a Site Collection**

```
Get-SPWorkflowConfig -SiteCollection "http://sp2013"
```

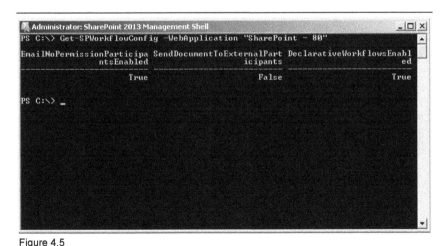

Figure 4.5

Get-SPWorkflowConfig displays the SharePoint workflow configuration settings.

41

Modifying SharePoint Workflow Configuration Settings

The Set-SPWorkflowConfig cmdlet allows you to modify the workflow configuration settings for a specific web application or site collection. Each setting, listed here, is a Boolean parameter:

- DeclarativeWorkflowsEnabled
- EmailNoPermissionParticipantsEnabled
- SendDocumentToExternalParticipants

A sample modification command line for a web application is shown in Listing 4.21. Modification of the site collection workflow configuration is shown in Listing 4.22.

LISTING 4.21 **Modifying the Workflow Settings for a Web Application**

```
Set-SPWorkflowConfig

-WebApplication "SharePoint Root Web App"

-DeclarativeWorkflowsEnabled:$false

-EmailNoPermissionParticipantsEnabled:$true

-SendDocumentToExternalParticipants:$true
```

LISTING 4.22 **Modifying the Workflow Settings for a Site Collection**

```
Set-SPWorkflowConfig

-SiteCollection "http://sp2013"

-DeclarativeWorkflowsEnabled:$true

-EmailNoPermissionParticipantsEnabled:$false
```

The DeclarativeWorkflowEnabled parameter determines whether users may define workflows from deployed managed code. The default value is True.

The EmailNoPermissionParticipantsEnabled parameter determines whether a user who does not have permissions to the site should receive an email if a task is assigned to him or her. The default value is True.

The SendDocumentToExternalParticipants parameter specifies whether external users should receive a copy of the workflow document. The default value is False.

These parameters correspond, respectively, to the workflow settings available in Central Administration, as shown in Figure 4.6.

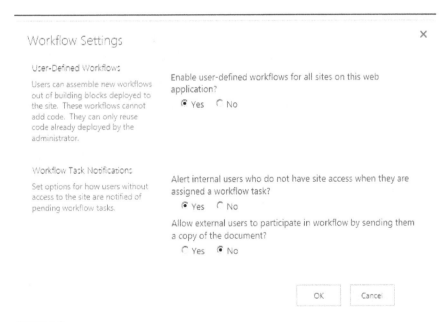

Figure 4.6

Workflow settings for a web application in Central Administration.

43

Displaying Available Timer Jobs on the SharePoint 2013 Farm

In order to obtain a timer job reference object, you need to find the identity of the timer job. Using Get-SPTimerJob by itself (see Listing 4.23) displays all available timer jobs, as shown in Figure 4.7.

LISTING 4.23 **Displaying All Available Timer Jobs**

```
Get-SPTimerJob
```

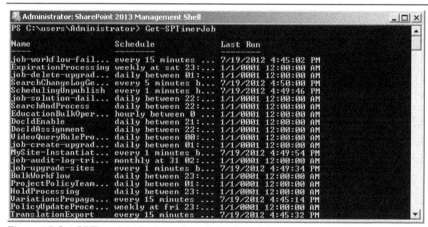

Figure 4.7 Get-SPTimerJob displays all available timer jobs.

Retrieving a Specific Timer Job

Providing the identity of the timer job with the Get-SPTimerJob cmdlet retrieves a specific timer job. Use this to assign the results to an object for use in other cmdlets, as shown in Listing 4.24.

LISTING 4.24 **Assigning a Variable to a Specific Timer Job**

```
$timerJob = Get-SPTimerJob -Identity "DocIDEnable"
```

The Identity parameter in this case is the name shown when retrieving all timer jobs (Get-SPTimerJob). You may also use the GUID of the timer job.

Enabling a Timer Job

To enable a timer job, execute the Enable-SPTimerJob cmdlet with the Identity of the timer job or a timer job variable. A sample command line is shown in Listing 4.25.

LISTING 4.25 **Enabling a Timer Job**

```
$timerJob = Get-SPTimerJob -Identity "DocIDEnable"
Enable-SPTimerJob $timerJob
```

Disabling a Timer Job

To disable a timer job, execute the Disable-SPTimerJob cmdlet with the Identity of the timer job or a timer job variable. A sample command line is shown in Listing 4.26.

LISTING 4.26 **Disabling a Timer Job**

```
$timerJob = Get-SPTimerJob -Identity "TimerJobID"
Disable-SPTimerJob $timerJob
```

Starting a Timer Job

To start a timer job, execute the Start-SPTimerJob cmdlet with the Identity of the timer job or a timer job variable. See the sample command line shown in Listing 4.27.

LISTING 4.27 **Starting a Timer Job**

```
$timerJob = Get-SPTimerJob -Identity "TimerJobID"
Start-SPTimerJob $timerJob
```

The timer job will kick off once when you start it manually. This is similar to clicking the Run Now button in Central Administration. However, you cannot start a timer job that is disabled. To insure kick-off, use the Enable-SPTimerJob cmdlet first to ensure that the timer job is enabled before attempting to start the job.

Setting the Schedule for a Timer Job

Setting the schedule for a timer job can be facilitated by using the Set-SPTimerJob cmdlet. Execute the Start-SPTimerJob cmdlet with the Identity of the timer job or a timer job variable along with the Schedule parameter. A sample command line is shown in Listing 4.28.

LISTING 4.28 **Setting the Schedule for a Timer Job**

```
$timerJob = Get-SPTimerJob -Identity "TimerJobID"
Set-SPTimerJob -Identity $timerJob -Schedule "Daily
at 21:00:00"
```

The Schedule parameter is a string value but must be in a schedule format:

- Every X minutes between 0 and 59.
- Hourly between 0 and 59.
- Daily at hh:mm:ss.
- Weekly between <day> hh:mm:ss and <day> hh:mm:ss. (<day> is the three letter day of the week (e.g. Sun, Mon, Tue, etc.)
- Monthly at dd hh:mm:ss.
- Yearly at <month> dd hh:mm:ss. (<month> is the three letter month e.g. Jan, Feb, Mar, etc.)

INTENTIONALLY BLANK

CHAPTER 5

Managing Web Applications

Displaying Available Web Applications

Using the Get-SPWebApplication without any parameters as shown in Listing 5.1 displays all available web applications as shown in Figure 5.1.

LISTING 5.1 **Display All Available Web Applications**

```
Get-SPWebApplication
```

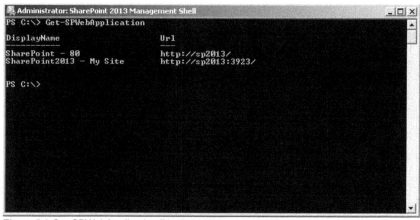

Figure 5.1 Get-SPWebApplication Displays All Available Web Applications

Getting a Specific Web Application Reference

Providing the identity of a particular web application with the Get-SPWebApplication cmdlet, retrieves a specific web application. Use this to assign the results to an object for use in other cmdlets as shown in Listing 5.2.

LISTING 5.2 **Assigning a Variable to a Specific Web Application**

```
$webApp = Get-SPWebApplication -Identity "PSWebApp"
```

You may use the URL or the Display Name of the web application as the Identity parameter value.

Removing a Web Application

The Remove-SPWebApplication cmdlet allows you to remove a specific web application from the current SharePoint farm. Use this cmdlet with the Get-SPWebApplication cmdlet as shown in Listing 5.3. You may also simply use the web application identity directly as shown in Listing 5.4.

LISTING 5.3 **Removing a Web Application using a Variable Example**

```
$webApp = Get-SPWebApplication -Identity "PSWebApp"
Remove-SPWebApplication $webApp
```

LISTING 5.4 **Removing a Web Application Directly**

```
Remove-SPWebApplication -Identity "PSWebApp"
```

You may use the –RemoveContentDatabases switch parameter to remove the web application content databases along with the web application itself.

Creating a New Web Application

To create a new web application, use the New-SPWebApplication cmdlet as follows:

```
New-SPWebApplication -applicationpool <name of new
application pool> -name <name of new web app> -
applicationpoolaccount <service account to be used
for the application pool> -port <desired port number>
```

An example command line entry for creating the main SharePoint web application is shown in Listing 5.5.

LISTING 5.5 **Creating a New Web Application**
```
New-SPWebApplication
-applicationpool NewWebApplication
-name NewWebApplication
-applicationpoolaccount SP\IISPoolAccount
-port 1234
```

After a few minutes, the display name and the URL of the new web application are presented in the console showing completion of the web application creation. If you do not provide a port number, a random port number is assigned, however, the first web application created on the SharePoint farm uses port 80.

Configuring Web Application Settings

Use Set-SPWebApplication to configure various web application settings. The Set-SPWebApplication has several parameter sets available. Therefore, executing the cmdlet the -? Parameter displays each parameter set as shown in Figure 5.2.

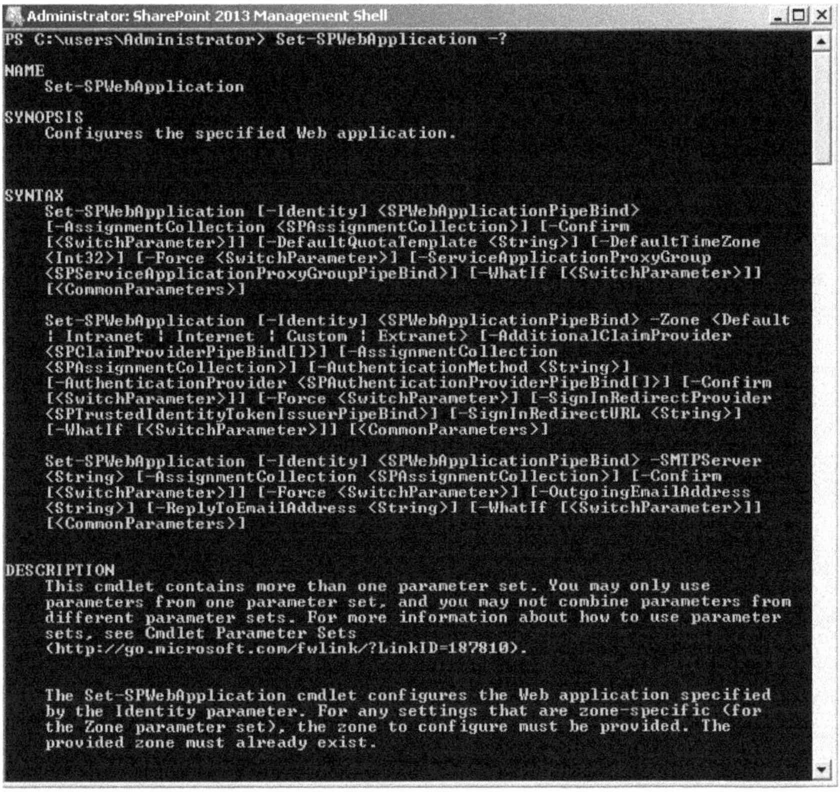

```
Administrator: SharePoint 2013 Management Shell
PS C:\users\Administrator> Set-SPWebApplication -?

NAME
    Set-SPWebApplication

SYNOPSIS
    Configures the specified Web application.


SYNTAX
    Set-SPWebApplication [-Identity] <SPWebApplicationPipeBind>
    [-AssignmentCollection <SPAssignmentCollection>] [-Confirm
    [<SwitchParameter>]] [-DefaultQuotaTemplate <String>] [-DefaultTimeZone
    <Int32>] [-Force <SwitchParameter>] [-ServiceApplicationProxyGroup
    <SPServiceApplicationProxyGroupPipeBind>] [-WhatIf [<SwitchParameter>]]
    [<CommonParameters>]

    Set-SPWebApplication [-Identity] <SPWebApplicationPipeBind> -Zone <Default
    | Intranet | Internet | Custom | Extranet> [-AdditionalClaimProvider
    <SPClaimProviderPipeBind[]>] [-AssignmentCollection
    <SPAssignmentCollection>] [-AuthenticationMethod <String>]
    [-AuthenticationProvider <SPAuthenticationProviderPipeBind[]>] [-Confirm
    [<SwitchParameter>]] [-Force <SwitchParameter>] [-SignInRedirectProvider
    <SPTrustedIdentityTokenIssuerPipeBind>] [-SignInRedirectURL <String>]
    [-WhatIf [<SwitchParameter>]] [<CommonParameters>]

    Set-SPWebApplication [-Identity] <SPWebApplicationPipeBind> -SMTPServer
    <String> [-AssignmentCollection <SPAssignmentCollection>] [-Confirm
    [<SwitchParameter>]] [-Force <SwitchParameter>] [-OutgoingEmailAddress
    <String>] [-ReplyToEmailAddress <String>] [-WhatIf [<SwitchParameter>]]
    [<CommonParameters>]


DESCRIPTION
    This cmdlet contains more than one parameter set. You may only use
    parameters from one parameter set, and you may not combine parameters from
    different parameter sets. For more information about how to use parameter
    sets, see Cmdlet Parameter Sets
    (http://go.microsoft.com/fwlink/?LinkID=187810).


    The Set-SPWebApplication cmdlet configures the Web application specified
    by the Identity parameter. For any settings that are zone-specific (for
    the Zone parameter set), the zone to configure must be provided. The
    provided zone must already exist.
```

Figure 5.2 Set-SPWebApplication Has Three Different Parameter Sets

Use the first parameter set to configure the Default Quota Template, the Default Time Zone, and/or the Service Application Proxy Group. Use the second parameter set to configure the Zone of the web application along with the associated authentication settings. The third parameter set may be used to configure various email settings for the web application selected web application.

Extending a Web Application

If you need to extend a web application to a different zone, use the New-SPWebApplicationExtension cmdlet. The New-SPWebApplicationExtension only requires the web application identity, the name of the new web site that will extend the web application, and the zone. The zone must not already be in use.

It is recommended to also include the new URL and HostHeader which the web application extension will use for the zone. An example command line entry for extending the main SharePoint web application is shown in Listing 5.5.

LISTING 5.6 **Extending a Web Application Example**

```
New-SPWebApplicationExtension
-Identity "SharePoint Root Site"
-Name "SP Internet Site"
-Zone Internet
-Url "http://internet"
-HostHeader "http://internet.sp2013.com"
```

The URL is the public facing http address while the HostHeader entry is the internal alternate access mapping. The Zone parameter may be one of the following:

- ▶ Default
- ▶ Intranet
- ▶ Internet
- ▶ Extranet
- ▶ Custom

Additional optional parameters are available to configure security and authentication.

Creating Alternate Access Mappings

You may programmatically generate alternate access mappings using the New-SPAlternateURL cmdlet. The main usage of this cmdlet requires the URL and the web application name as shown in Listing 5.7.

LISTING 5.7 **Creating an Alternate Access Mapping**

```
New-SPAlternateURL -URL "http://intranet.sp2013.com"
-WebApplication "SharePoint Root Site" -Internal -
Zone Intranet
```

To create the mapping for internal use, use the –Internal switch parameter, otherwise a public URL entry is created. Use the –Zone parameter to specify the zone. The valid zone values are:

- Default
- Intranet
- Internet
- Extranet
- Custom

Displaying Current Alternate Access Mappings

Use the Get-SPAlternateURL without any parameters to display the current URL mappings of the SharePoint 2013 farm as shown in Listing 5.8.

LISTING 5.8 **Example Command to Display All Alternate URLs**

```
Get-SPAlternateURL
```

Retrieving a Specific Alternate URL Mapping

Providing the identity of the alternate URL with the Get-SPAlternateURL cmdlet, retrieves a specific alternate access mapping instance. Use this to assign the results to a variable for use in other cmdlets as shown in Listing 5.9.

LISTING 5.9 **Assigning a Variable to a Specific Alternate URL Entry**

```
$altURL = Get-SPAlternateURL -Identity
"http://intranet.sp2013.com"
```

Changing the Zone of an Alternate Access Mapping

The Set-SPAlternateURL allows you to configure the zone of a specific alternate access mapping entry. This is the only setting that may be modified using the Set-SPAlternateURL cmdlet.

An example command line is shown in Listing 5.10.

LISTING 5.10 **Changing the Zone of an Alternate Access Mapping**

```
Set-SPAlternateURL -Identity
"http://intranet.sp2013.com" -Zone Intranet
```

The –Identity parameter can be the Incoming URL or an alternate access mapping object variable. If the alternate access mapping entry is public and the zone is Default, you may not change the zone until another public entry is created for the Default zone.

Removing an Alternate Access Mapping

The Remove-SPAlternateURL cmdlet allows you to remove the specified alternate URL entry. The only required parameter is the Identity of the URL mapping as shown in Listing 5.11.

LISTING 5.11 **Remova an Existing Alternate Access Mapping**

```
Remove-SPAlternateURL
-Identity "http://intranet.sp2013.com"
```

The –Identity parameter can be the Incoming URL or an alternate access mapping object variable. If the alternate access mapping entry is public and the zone is Default, you may not remove the alternate access mapping entry.

INTENTIONALLY BLANK

CHAPTER 6

Managing Service Applications

Installing Service Applications

Using the Install-SPService cmdlet installs all service applications on a server based on the services, service proxies, and service instances stored in the local registry. Using the –Provision switch parameter allows the service applications to be installed using the default settings as shown in Listing 6.1.

LISTING 6.1 **Installing All Available Service Applications**

```
Install-SPService -Provision
```

Displaying Available Service Applications on the current SharePoint 2013 Farm

Using the Get-SPServiceApplication without any parameters as shown in Listing 6.2 displays all available service applications on the current SharePoint 2013 farm as shown in Figure 6.1.

LISTING 6.2 **Display All Available Service Applications**

```
Get-SPServiceApplication
```

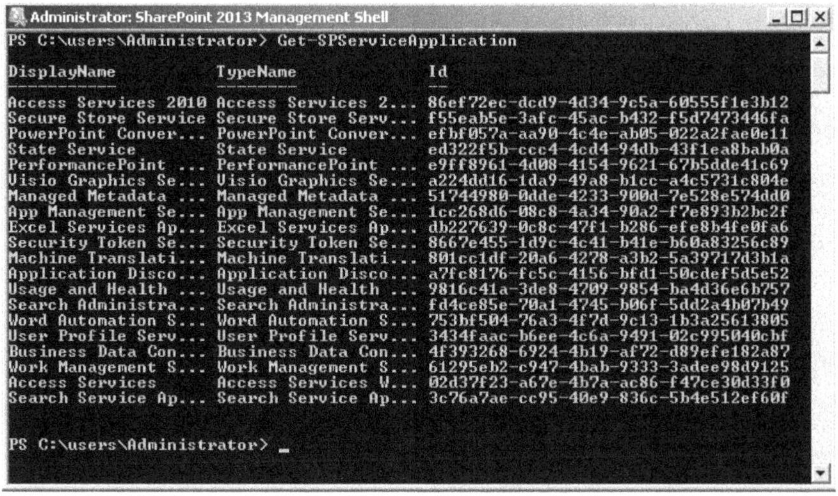

Figure 6.1 Get-SPService Application Displays All Available Service Applications

Retrieving a Specific Service Application

Providing the identity or the name of a particular service application with the Get-SPServiceApplication cmdlet, retrieves a specific service application. Use this to assign the results to an object for use in other cmdlets as shown in Listing 6.3.

LISTING 6.3 **Assigning a Variable to a Specific Service Application**

```
$sApp = Get-SPServiceApplication
-Identity bc4399ed-a2e0-4397-bf07-cd3d207e630e
```

As mentioned above, you may use the -Name parameter and provide the name of the service application instead of using the - Identity with the service application GUID.

Configuring IIS Settings for a Service Application

The Set-SPServiceApplication cmdlet allows you to set the default end point, the application pool, and/or the service proxy for a specific service application. Use this in conjunction with the Get-SPServiceApplication cmdlet (explained in the previous section) as shown in Listing 6.4.

LISTING 6.4 **Example Configuration Script for a Service Application**

```
$sApp = Get-SPServiceApplication
     -Identity bc4399ed-a2e0-4397-bf07-cd3d207e630e
Set-SPServiceApplication $sApp
     -IISWebServiceApplicationPool
     "ServiceApplicationPool"
```

The main parameters for configuring a service application with the Set-SPServiceApplication cmdlet are:

- DefaultEndPoint
- IISWebServiceApplicationPool
- ServiceApplicationProxyGroup

Sharing a Service Application Between Farms

The Publish-SPServiceApplication cmdlet allows you to make a specific service application available outside of the current farm. Use this in conjunction with the Get-SPServiceApplication cmdlet as shown in Listing 6.6.

LISTING 6.6 **Example Configuration Script for Sharing a Service Application**

```
$sApp = Get-SPServiceApplication
     -Identity bc4399ed-a2e0-4397-bf07-cd3d207e630e
Publish-SPServiceApplication $sApp
```

Removing a Service Application

The Remove-SPServiceApplication cmdlet allows you to remove a specific service application from the current SharePoint farm. Use this in conjunction with the Get-SPServiceApplication cmdlet as shown in Listing 6.7.

LISTING 6.7 **Example Configuration Script for Removing a Service Application**

```
$sApp = Get-SPServiceApplication
      -Identity bc4399ed-a2e0-4397-bf07-cd3d207e630e

Remove-SPServiceApplication $sApp
```

Displaying the Service Instances on a Server

Using the Get-SPServiceInstance with the Server parameter, as shown in Listing 6.8, displays all available service applications as shown in Figure 6.2.

LISTING 6.8 **Display All Available Service Instances Example**

```
Get-SPServiceInstance -Server sp2013svr03
```

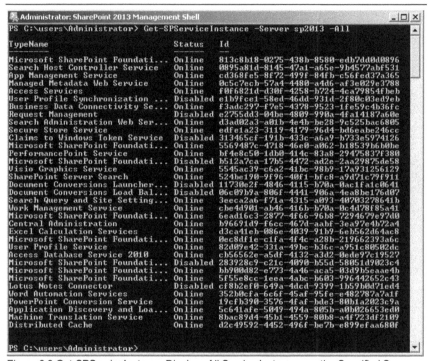

Figure 6.2 Get-SPServiceInstance Displays All Service Instances on the Specified Server

If the Server parameter is not provided, the cmdlet displays all service instances within the current SharePoint 2013 farm.

Retrieving a Specific Service Instance

Providing the identity of a particular service instance with the Get-SPServiceInstance cmdlet, retrieves a specific service instance. Use this to assign the results to an object for use in other cmdlets as shown in Listing 6.9.

LISTING 6.9 **Assigning a Variable to a Specific Service Instance**

```
$serviceInst = Get-SPServiceInstance
        -Identity 5fedc699-7810-4157-9c59-19f7d6e67e38
```

Start a Service Instance

The Start-SPServiceInstance cmdlet starts the specified service on the current server. You may provide the identity directly to the cmdlet or use a variable as shown in Listing 6.10.

LISTING 6.10 **Starting a Service Instance**

```
$serviceInst = Get-SPServiceInstance -Identity
5fedc699-7810-4157-9c59-19f7d6e67e38
Start-SPServiceInstance $serviceInst
```

Stopping a Service Instance

The Stop-SPServiceInstance cmdlet stops the specified service on the current server. You may provide the identity directly to the cmdlet or use a variable as shown in Listing 6.11.

LISTING 6.11 **Stopping a Service Instance**

```
$serviceInst = Get-SPServiceInstance
        -Identity 5fedc699-7810-4157-9c59-19f7d6e67e38

Stop-SPServiceInstance $serviceInst
```

CHAPTER 7

Managing the SharePoint 2013 Databases

Displaying All SharePoint Databases

In order to obtain a database reference object, you need to find the identity of the database. Using the Get-SPDatabase cmdlet with the ServerInstance parameter (see Listing 7.1) displays all available databases, as shown in Figure 7.1.

You need to pass in the SQL Server instance to the ServerInstance parameter. This is not any of the SharePoint servers.

LISTING 7.1 **Display All Databases Example**

```
Get-SPDatabase -ServerInstance "SP2013\SQLSharePoint"
```

FIGURE 7.1

The Get-SPDatabase –ServerInstance cmdlet displays all databases on the SQL Server.

Retrieving a Specific Database

Providing the identity of the database with the Get-SPDatabase cmdlet retrieves a specific database. Use this to assign the results to an object for use in other cmdlets, as shown in Listing 7.2.

LISTING 7.2 **Assigning a Variable to a Specific Database**

```
$database = Get-SPDatabase

  -Identity 47036154-7a05-44be-9137-9be09f43ccb5
```

Creating a New Content Database

The New-SPContentDatabase cmdlet allows you to create a new content database using -Name and -WebApplication parameters as shown in Listing 7.3.

LISTING 7.3 **Creating a New Content Database Example**

```
New-SPContentDatabase -Name NewContentDB -
WebApplication "PSWebApp"
```

After a few minutes, creation is confirmed by an output of the content database information, as shown in Figure 7.2.

FIGURE 7.2
Content database information is displayed after creation.

Displaying All Content Databases for a Web Application

Using the WebApplication parameter with the Get-SPContentDatabase cmdlet, as shown in Listing 7.4, will display information about all content databases associated to the specified web application, as shown in Figure 7.3.

LISTING 7.4 **Displaying All Content Databases for a Web Application**

```
Get-SPContentDatabase -WebApplication "PSWebApp"
```

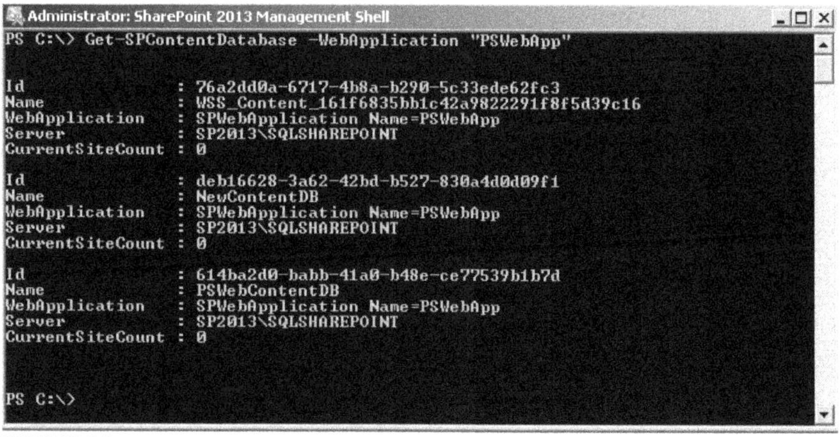

FIGURE 7.3
Results of using the Get-SPContentDatabase cmdlet with the WebApplication parameter

Detaching a Content Database from a Web Application

The Dismount-SPContentDatabase cmdlet allows you to dissociate the specified content database with the web application without removing the underlying database itself. Use this in conjunction with the Get-SPContentDatabase cmdlet, as shown in Listing 7.5.

LISTING 7.5 **Sample Script for Detaching a Content Database**

```
$database = Get-SPContentDatabase
     -Identity 025b1239-cd62-451e-943d-dff2e0d52ec8
Dismount-SPContentDatabase $database
```

Attaching a Content Database to a Web Application

The Mount-SPContentDatabase cmdlet allows you to attach the specified content database to a particular web application. The command-line entry is similar to creating a new content database using the -Name and -WebApplication parameters , as shown in Listing 7.6.

LISTING 7.6 **Sample Script for Attaching a Content Database**

```
Mount-SPContentDatabase

    -Name "NewContentDatabase"

    -WebApplication "PowerShellWebApp"
```

Deleting a Content Database

The Remove-SPContentDatabase cmdlet allows you to delete the specified content database as shown in Listing 7.7.

LISTING 7.7 **Sample Script for Deleting a Content Database**

```
$database = Get-SPContentDatabase
        -Identity 025b1239-cd62-451e-943d-dff2e0d52ec8


Remove-SPContentDatabase $database
```

Creating a New Configuration Database

The New-SPConfigurationDatabase cmdlet allows you to create a new configuration database using the DatabaseName and DatabaseServer parameters. A sample command-line entry is show in Listing 7.8.

LISTING 7.8 **Creating a New Configuration Database**

```
New-SPConfigurationDatabase

       -DatabaseName NewConfigurationDB

       -DatabaseServer "SP2013\SQLSharePoint"
```

The farm credentials and a passphrase are needed to execute this cmdlet. If you do not provide these in line with the cmdlet, you will be prompted to provide this information.

Deleting a Configuration Database

The Remove-SPConfigurationDatabase cmdlet allows you to delete the current configuration database. You do not need to pass any parameters into this cmdlet, as shown in Listing 7.9.

LISTING 7.9 **Sample Script for Deleting a Configuration Database**

```
Remove-SPConfigurationDatabase
```

Backing Up a Configuration Database

The Backup-SPConfigurationDatabase cmdlet allows you to per-form a backup on a configuration database, placing the backup files in the directory specified. An example is shown in Listing 7.10.

LISTING 7.10 **Sample Script for Backing Up a Configuration Database**

```
Backup-SPConfigurationDatabase -Directory H:\Backups
```

The default configuration database is the database being used by the current SharePoint farm, however, the –DatabaseServer and –DatabaseName parameters may be used to specify a particular con-figuration database name and location.

If you are backing up the current configuration database being used by the farm, you may also use the Backup-SPFarm cmdlet with the ConfigurationOnly switch parameter, as shown in Listing 7.11.

LISTING 7.11 **Using Backup-SPFarm to Back Up the Configuration Data-base**

```
Backup-SPFarm

        -BackupMethod Full

        -Directory H:\Backups

        -ConfigurationOnly
```

The BackupMethod parameter can be either Full or Differential. Full will back up the entire configuration, whereas Differential on-ly backs up changes that have occurred since the last full backup was performed.

Restoring a Configuration Database

The Restore-SPFarm cmdlet allows you to restore a configuration database based on the backup files in the directory specified. Use the –ConfigurationOnly switch parameter to only restore the configuration database, as shown in Listing 7.12.

LISTING 7.12 **Sample Script for Restoring a Configuration Database**

```
Restore-SPFarm

    -Directory H:\Backups

    -ConfigurationOnly

    -RestoreMethod Overwrite
```

The RestoreMethod parameter can be New or Overwrite. Using New creates a new location for the backup to be restored. Overwrite will restore the backup in place and overwrite the current configuration.

Backing Up a SharePoint 2013 Farm

The Backup-SPFarm cmdlet allows you to perform a backup of the entire farm (or item in the farm), placing the backup files in the directory specified. An example is shown in Listing 7.13.

LISTING 7.13 **Sample Script for Backing Up the SharePoint Farm**

```
Backup-SPFarm

-BackupMethod Full

-Directory H:\Backups
```

The BackupMethod parameter can be either Full or Differential. Full will back up the entire configuration, whereas Differential only backs up changes that have occurred since the last full backup was performed.

Run Backup-SPFarm with the −ShowTree parameter to display all items in the farm that may be backed up. Use the −Item parameter with Backup-SPFarm to back up a specific item in the farm.

Restoring a SharePoint 2013 Farm

The Restore-SPFarm cmdlet allows you to restore the farm based on the backup files in the directory specified, as shown in Listing 7.14.

LISTING 7.14 **Sample Script for Restoring a SharePoint Farm**

```
Restore-SPFarm −Directory H:\Backups −RestoreMethod
Overwrite
```

The RestoreMethod parameter can be New or Overwrite. Using New creates a new location for the backup to be restored. Overwrite will restore the backup in place and overwrite the current farm content.

Backing Up a Site Collection

The Backup-SPSite cmdlet allows you to perform a backup of a specific site collection, creating a backup file based on the path specified. An example is shown in Listing 7.15.

LISTING 7.15 **Sample Script for Backing Up a Site Collection**

```
Backup-SPSite

-Identity "http://sp2013/sites/SearchCenter"

-Path H:\Backups\SearchCenter.bak
```

The Identity parameter can be the URL or the GUID of the site collection. Using the URL is usually easier. The Path parameter defines where the backup will be stored, along with the name of the backup file to create.

Restoring a Site Collection

The Restore-SPSite cmdlet allows you to restore a site collection based on the backup file in the path specified, as shown in Listing 7.16.

LISTING 7.16 **Sample Script for Restoring a Site Collection**

```
Restore-SPSite
-Identity "http://sp2013/sites/SearchCenter"
-Path H:\Backups\SearchCenter.bak
-Force
```

The Force switch parameter is needed to overwrite an existing site collection. You may also specify the DatabaseName and DatabaseServer parameters to specify where the content of the site collection should be stored.

PART III

Site Management and Administration

INTENTIONALLY BLANK

CHAPTER 8

Managing Site Collections and Subsites

Displaying All Available Site Collections on the SharePoint 2013 Farm

Using the Get-SPSite cmdlet without any parameters as shown in Listing 8.1 displays all available site collections, as shown in Figure 8.1.

LISTING 8.1 **Displaying All Available Site Collections**

```
Get-SPSite
```

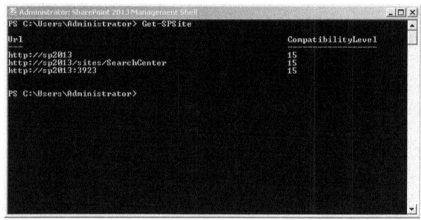

FIGURE 8.1
The Get-SPSite cmdlet displays all available sites.

Displaying Available Site Collections in a Specific Web Application

Using the Get-SPSite cmdlet with the WebApplication parameter, as shown in Listing 8.2, displays all available site collections in the specified web application.

LISTING 8.2 **Displaying Available Site Collections in a Web Application**

```
Get-SPSite -WebApplication "SharePoint - 80"
```

Displaying Available Site Collections in a Specific Content Database

Using the Get-SPSite cmdlet with the ContentDatabase parameter, as shown in Listing 8.3, displays all available site collections in the specified content database.

LISTING 8.3 **Displaying Available Site Collections in a Content Database**

```
Get-SPSite -ContentDatabase "WSS_TEAMSITES_CONTENTDB"
```

Retrieving a Specific Site Collection

Providing the identity of the site collection with the Get-SPSite cmdlet retrieves a specific site collection. Use this to assign the results to an object for use in other cmdlets, as shown in Listing 8.4.

LISTING 8.4 **Assigning a Variable to a Specific Site Collection**

```
$siteCol = Get-SPSite -Identity "http://sp2013"
```

Deleting a Site Collection

The Remove-SPSite cmdlet allows you to delete a specific site collection from the current server. Use this in conjunction with the Get-SPSite cmdlet (explained in a previous section), as shown in Listing 8.5, or just use the site collection identity directly in line, as shown in Listing 8.6.

LISTING 8.5 **Removing a Site Collection Using a Variable**

```
$siteCol = Get-SPSite
      -Identity "http://sp2013/sites/sitecol"

Remove-SPSite $siteCol
```

LISTING 8.6 **Removing a Site Collection Directly**

```
Remove-SPSite -Identity "http://sp2013/sites/sitecol"
```

The Remove-SPSite cmdlet has an optional switch parameter named GradualDelete. Using this parameter will remove the site collection and any subsites underneath gradually. This helps keeps the SharePoint load down and therefore is highly recommended for large site collections.

Creating a Site Collection

To create a new site collection, use the New-SPSite cmdlet as follows:

```
New-SPSite

    -url <full url of new site collection>

    -name <name of new site collection>

    -owneralias <site collection administrator>

    -template <site collection template to use>
```

A sample command-line entry for creating the root site collection using the Team Site template is shown in Listing 8.7.

LISTING 8.7 **Creating a New Site Collection**

```
New-SPSite

    -url http://sp2013/sites/sitecol

    -name Home

    -owneralias SP\SiteColAdmin

    -template STS#0
```

The site template names can be found using Get-SPWebTemplates. If no template is provided, the site collection will still be created. In this case, once the site is accessed via the browser, SharePoint will prompt for a site collection template to be selected.

Locking a Site Collection

Using the -LockState parameter with the Set-SPSite cmdlet allows you to lock or unlock the site collection. The following are valid values for the LockState parameter:

- Unlock
- NoAdditions
- ReadOnly
- NoAccess

The Unlock state allows full availability to users (based on the normal permissions). NoAdditions allows you to lock the site collection such that no new content may be added. This does not lock down updates or deletes.

To fully lock down the content, use the ReadOnly state. Placing the site collection into the ReadOnly state prevents users from adding, updating, or deleting content.

NoAccess disables all access to the site collection. Users will not even be able to navigate to the site collection location (or locations underneath).

A sample command line for changing the lock state is shown in Listing 8.8.

LISTING 8.8 **Changing the Lock State of a Site Collection**

```
Set-SPSite

-Identity http://sp2013/sites/sitecol

-LockState NoAdditions
```

Setting Storage Limits on a Site Collection

To set the storage limits on a site collection use MaxSize and WarningSize with the Set-SPSite cmdlet as shown in Listing 8.9.

LISTING 8.9 **Setting the Storage Limits on a Site Collection**

```
Set-SPSite

    -Identity http://sp2013/sites/sitecol

    -MaxSize 1024

    -WarningSize 768
```

The units for both parameter values are in megabytes. The MaxSize parameter can be any integer value but must be greater than or equal to the WarningSize value. Therefore, the Warning-Size parameter can be any value between zero and the MaxSize value.

Creating a Site within a Site Collection

To create a new subsite within a site collection, use the New-SPWeb cmdlet as follows:

```
New-SPWeb

    -url <full url of new site>

    -name <name of new site>

    -template <site template to use>
```

The following switch parameters are available when you are using the New-SPWeb cmdlet:

- AddToTopNav
- UniquePermissions
- UseParentTopNav

The AddToTopNav switch parameter places the new site within the top navigation of the site collection. Using the UseParentTopNav switch parameter replicates the top nav of the site collection onto the new subsite.

Creating a site with UniquePermissions forces the site to not inherit permissions from the site collection and only grants the System Account Full Control access.

A sample command-line entry for creating a subsite using the Team Site template is shown in Listing 8.10.

LISTING 8.10 **Creating a Site Under a Site Collection**

```
New-SPWeb
      -url http://sp2013/sites/sitecol/newsubsite
      -name "New Sub Site"
      -template STS#0
      -AddToTopNav
      -UniquePermissions
      -UseParentTopNav
```

The site template names can be found using Get-SPWebTemplates. If no template is provided, the site will still be created. In this case, once the site is accessed via the browser, SharePoint will prompt for a site template to be selected.

Displaying All Subsites within a Site Collection

To display all subsites within a site collection, you need to use the Get-SPWeb cmdlet with the Identity parameter. If you only provide the site collection URL, Get-SPWeb will only return the site collection web object. Therefore, you need to provide a wildcard path, as shown in Listing 8.11.

LISTING 8.11 **Displaying All Subsites Within a Site Collection**

```
Get-SPWeb -Identity "http://sp2013/sites/sitecol/*"
```

You may also use the Site parameter instead of the wildcard Identity parameter to retrieve all webs, including the site collection web. A sample command line is shown in Listing 8.12.

LISTING 8.12 **Displaying All Webs Within a Site Collection**

```
Get-SPWeb -Site "http://sp2013/sites/sitecol"
```

Retrieving a Specific Subsite

Providing the identity of the subsite with the Get-SPWeb cmdlet retrieves a specific subsite. Use this to assign the results to an object for use in other cmdlets, as shown in Listing 8.13.

LISTING 8.13 **Assigning a Variable to a Specific Subsite**

```
$web = Get-SPWeb -Identity
"http://sp2013/sites/sitecol/subsite"
```

Deleting a Subsite from a Site Collection

The Remove-SPWeb cmdlet allows you to delete a specific sub-site. Use this in conjunction with the Get-SPWeb cmdlet, as shown in Listing 8.14, or just use the path identity directly in line, as shown in Listing 8.15.

LISTING 8.14 **Removing a Subsite Application Using a Variable**

```
$web = Get-SPWeb
     -Identity "http://sp2013/sites/sitecol/subsite"



Remove-SPWeb $web
```

LISTING 8.15 **Removing a Subsite Directly**

```
Remove-SPWeb


     -Identity "http://sp2013/sites/sitecol/subsite"
```

Modifying the URL of a Subsite

You may easily change the name of the relative URL in which a subsite is accessed by using the Set-SPWeb cmdlet. Provide the URL of the site as the Identity parameter and use the RelativeURL parameter to provide the new URL, as shown in Listing 8.16.

LISTING 8.16 **Modifying the URL of a Subsite**

```
Set-SPWeb
-Identity "http://sp2013/sites/sitecol/newsubsite"

-RelativeURL departments
```

Moving a Site Collection to a Different Content Database

The Move-SPSite cmdlet allows you to move a site collection from one content database to another. All that is needed to execute this cmdlet is the site collection identity and the destination database name. A sample command line is shown in Listing 8.17.

LISTING 8.17 **Moving a Site Collection to a Different Content Database**

```
Move-SPSite
-Identity "http://sp2013/sites/sitecol"
-DestinationDatabase "WSS_DEPARTMENTS_CONTENTDB"
```

You do not need to provide the originating database because there is no parameter for that anyway. The destination database must already exist.

Moving All Site Collections from One Content Database to Another

You may pipe the results of Get-SPSite to the Move-SPSite cmdlet. Therefore, by using the ContentDatabase parameter with Get-SPSite, you may move all site collections from that content database to a new content database. A sample command line is shown in Listing 8.18.

LISTING 8.18 **Moving All Site Collections From a Content Database**

```
Get-SPSite -ContentDatabase "WSS_CONTENT" | Move-
SPSite
-DestinationDatabase "WSS_DEPARTMENTS_CONTENTDB"
```

Similar to moving a single site collection, the destination database must already exist.

Displaying Deleted Site Collections

In order to obtain a deleted site collection reference object, you need to find the URL (Identity) or SiteId of the site collection. Using the Get-SPDeletedSite cmdlet displays all deleted site collections as shown in Figure 8.2.

FIGURE 8.2
The Get-SPDeletedSite cmdlet displays all deleted sites.

Displaying Deleted Site Collections in a Specific Content Database

Using the Get-SPDeletedSite cmdlet with the ContentDatabase parameter, as shown in Listing 8.19, displays all deleted site collections in the specified content database.

LISTING 8.19 **Displaying Deleted Site Collections in a Content Database**

```
Get-SPDeletedSite -ContentDatabase "WSS_CONTENT"
```

Retrieving a Specific Deleted Site Collection

Providing the identity of the deleted site collection with the Get-SPDeletedSite cmdlet retrieves a specific site collection. Use this to assign the results to an object for use in other cmdlets, as shown in Listing 8.20.

LISTING 8.20 **Assigning a Variable to a Specific Deleted Site Collection**

```
$deletedSiteCol = Get-SPDeletedSite -Identity
"/sites/deletedsitecol"
```

Removing a Deleted Site Collection

The Remove-SPDeletedSite cmdlet allows you to remove a specific deleted site collection from the current server. Use this in conjunction with the Get-SPDeletedSite cmdlet (explained in a previous section), as shown in Listing 8.21, or just use the site collection identity directly in line, as shown in Listing 8.22.

93

LISTING 8.21 **Removing a Site Collection Using a Variable**

```
$deletedSiteCol = Get-SPDeletedSite -Identity "/
sites/ deletedsitecol "
Remove-SPDeletedSite $deletedSiteCol
```

LISTING 8.22 **Removing a Deleted Site Collection Directly**

```
Remove-SPDeletedSite -Identity "
/sites/deletedsitecol"
```

Restoring a Deleted Site Collection

The Restore-SPDeletedSite cmdlet allows you to restore a deleted site collection from the current SharePoint 2013 farm. Use this in conjunction with the Get-SPDeletedSite cmdlet (explained in a previous section), as shown in Listing 8.23, or just use the site collection identity directly in line, as shown in Listing 8.24.

LISTING 8.23 **Restoring a Deleted Site Collection Using a Variable**

```
$deletedSiteCol = Get-SPDeletedSite -Identity
"/sites/deletedsitecol"
Restore-SPDeletedSite $deletedSiteCol
```

LISTING 8.24 **Restoring a Deleted Site Collection Directly**

```
Restore-SPDeletedSite -Identity
"/sites/deletedsitecol"
```

Configuring Information Rights Management (IRM) Settings for a Site

This chapter covers the basic or more common Site Management cmdlets. However, SharePoint 2013 provides advance scripting for IRM settings. As such, the following cmdlets nouns are now available:

▶ SPIRMSettings

▶ SPSiteSubscriptionIRMConfig

INTENTIONALLY BLANK

CHAPTER 9

Managing Solutions and Features

Adding a Solution to the SharePoint 2013 Farm

Using the Add-SPSolution cmdlet adds a solution package (.wsp) to the farm. All you need to provide the cmdlet is the actual location of the solution package, as shown in Listing 9.1.

LISTING 9.1 **Adding a Solution to the SharePoint 2013Farm**

```
Add-SPSolution "e:\deploy\SP2013Solution.wsp"
```

The solution location is the –LiteralPath parameter, which is required. The path may be a local drive location or network location using a UNC string (\\servername\folder).

Displaying Available Solutions on the SharePoint 2013 Farm

In order to obtain a solution reference object, you need to find the identity of the solution. Using the Get-SPSolution cmdlet by itself (see Listing 9.2) displays all available solutions deployed to the current farm.

LISTING 9.2 **Displaying All Available Solutions**

```
Get-SPSolution
```

Retrieving a Specific Solution

Providing the identity of the solution with the Get-SPSolution cmdlet retrieves a specific solution. Use this to assign the results to an object for use in other cmdlets, as shown in Listing 9.3.

LISTING 9.3 **Assigning a Variable to a Specific Solution**

```
$solution = Get-SPSolution

-Identity d1f42bdf-736e-2e3b-2bc3-e2f876b233fe
```

Deploying a Solution to a Web Application

The Install-SPSolution cmdlet allows you to deploy a specific solution installed on the farm to a specified web application. Use this in conjunction with the Get-SPSolution cmdlet (explained in a previous section), as shown in Listing 9.4.

LISTING 9.4 **Sample Configuration Script for Deploying a Solution**

```
$solution = Get-SPSolution

    -Identity d1f42bdf-736e-2e3b-2bc3-e2f876b233fe

Install-SPSolution $solution

    -WebApplication "SharePoint Root Web"

    -Force

    -GACDeployment
```

The –Force switch parameter forces the solution to be deployed to the specified web application. As noted, if there are no components scoped for the web application level, you cannot even force the solution to be deployed to the web application. However, if you are deploying the solution globally, the –Force parameter will redeploy the solution if it has already been previously deployed.

The –GACDeployment switch parameter needs to be included if there are assemblies in the solution that will be deployed to the Global Assembly Cache (GAC). Most of the time this is the case—especially with third-party products.

If code access security (CAS) policies are included in the solution, you need to provide the –CASPolicies switch parameter to the Install-SPSolution command. This is less common but does occur.

Retracting a Deployed Solution

The Uninstall-SPSolution cmdlet allows you to retract a specific solution that was previously deployed. Use this in conjunction with the Get-SPSolution cmdlet (explained in a previous section), as shown in Listing 9.5.

LISTING 9.5 **Retracting a Solution from a Web Application**

```
$solution = Get-SPSolution

-Identity d1f42bdf-736e-2e3b-2bc3-e2f876b233fe

Uninstall-SPSolution $solution -WebApplication
"SharePoint - 80"
```

Providing the –WebApplication parameter retracts the solution from the specified web application (assuming the solution was deployed to that web application and has resources scoped at the web application level). You may also retract the solution from all web applications, as shown in Listing 9.6.

LISTING 9.6 **Retracting a Solution from All Web Applications**

```
$solution = Get-SPSolution

       -Identity d1f42bdf-736e-2e3b-2bc3-e2f876b233fe

Uninstall-SPSolution $solution -AllWebApplications
```

If the solution is installed globally, all you need to provide to the Uninstall-SPSolution cmdlet is the solution identity, as shown in Listing 9.7

.

LISTING 9.7 **Retracting a Solution That Was Globally Deployed**

```
$solution = Get-SPSolution

-Identity d1f42bdf-736e-2e3b-2bc3-e2f876b233fe

Uninstall-SPSolution $solution
```

Upgrading a Deployed Solution

The Update-SPSolution cmdlet allows you to upgrade a previously deployed solution with a newer version of the solution package (and underlying files). Use this in conjunction with the Get-SPSolution cmdlet (explained in a previous section), as shown in Listing 9.8.

LISTING 9.8 **Sample Configuration Script for Upgrading a Solution**

```
$solution = Get-SPSolution

    -Identity d1f42bdf-736e-2e3b-2bc3-e2f876b233fe

Update-SPSolution $solution

    -LiteralPath "E:\DEPLOY\newsolution.wsp"

    -Force

    -GACDeployment
```

The –LiteralPath determines the location of the updated solution package. The path may be a local drive location or network location using a UNC string (\\servername\folder).

The –Force switch parameter forces the solution to be upgraded.

The –GACDeployment switch parameter needs to be included if there are assemblies in the solution that will be redeployed to the Global Assembly Cache (GAC).

If code access security (CAS) policies are included in the solution, you need to provide the –CASPolicies switch parameter to the Update-SPSolution command.

102

Removing a Solution from the SharePoint 2013 Farm

The Remove-SPSolution cmdlet allows you to remove a specific solution from the current farm. Use this in conjunction with the Get-SPSolution cmdlet (explained in a previous section), as shown in Listing 9.9.

LISTING 9.9 **Sample Configuration Script for Removing a Solution**

```
$solution = Get-SPSolution
-Identity d1f42bdf-736e-2e3b-2bc3-e2f876b233fe


Remove-SPSolution $solution
```

Displaying Available Features in SharePoint 2013

The Get-SPFeature cmdlet is handy for listing out the installed features at various levels within your SharePoint environment. Issuing the command without any parameters displays all features at every level.

The Get-SPFeature cmdlet has several parameter sets you may use to narrow your list of features. To display the features at the farm level, simply use the –Farm switch parameter, as shown in Listing 9.10.

LISTING 9.10 **Displaying All Installed Farm Features**

```
Get-SPFeature -Farm
```

To display the features at the web application level, use the –WebApplication parameter and provide the web application name or identity, as shown in Listing 9.11.

LISTING 9.11 **Displaying All Installed Web Application Features**

```
Get-SPFeature -WebApplication "SharePoint - 80"
```

This also works for site collection and site features as well. For site collections, use the –Site parameter (see Listing 9.12) and for site features use the –Web parameter (see Listing 9.13).

LISTING 9.12 **Displaying All Installed Site Collection Features**

```
Get-SPFeature -Site "http://sp2013"
```

LISTING 9.13 **Displaying All Installed Site Features**

```
Get-SPFeature -Web "http://sp2013"
```

Retrieving a Specific Feature

Providing the identity of the solution with the Get-SPSolution cmdlet retrieves a specific solution. Use this to assign the results to an object for use in other cmdlets, as shown in Listing 9.14.

LISTING 9.14 **Assigning a Variable to a Specific Feature**

```
$feature = Get-SPFeature

-Identity f3382bc7-93bc-8325-b1c5-7dba9034c7b2
```

Activating a Feature

The Enable-SPFeature cmdlet allows you to activate a feature at the determined level. Use this in conjunction with the Get-SPFeature cmdlet (explained in the previous section), as shown in Listing 9.15.

LISTING 9.15 **Sample Script for Activating a Feature**

```
$feature = Get-SPFeature

  -Identity f3382bc7-93bc-8325-b1c5-7dba9034c7b2

Enable-SPFeature $feature -Url "http://sp2013" -Force
```

The –Url parameter is the web application, site collection, or site in which the feature should be activated. At the root level of the main site, the address is the same. Features can only be activated at the level in which they reside.

The –Force switch parameter forces the activation and reruns any customized code. This occurs if the feature is already activated and you are forcing a "reactivation."

Deactivating a Feature

The Disable-SPFeature cmdlet allows you to deactivate a feature at the determined level. Use this in conjunction with the Get-SPFeature cmdlet (explained in a previous section), as shown in Listing 9.16.

LISTING 9.16 **Sample Script for Deactivating a Feature**

```
$feature = Get-SPFeature

   -Identity f3382bc7-93bc-8325-b1c5-7dba9034c7b2

Disable-SPFeature $feature

      -Url "http://sp2013"

      -Force
```

The –Url parameter is the web application, site collection, or site in which the feature should be activated. At the root level of the main site, the address is the same. Features can only be deactivated at the level in which they reside and are activated.

The –Force switch parameter forces the deactivation and does not produce any errors if the feature is already deactivated.

Installing a Feature

The Install-SPFeature cmdlet allows you to install a feature that already has been copied or deployed to the SharePoint environment. The feature files should reside within a folder under the 15\TEMPLATE\FEATURES location of the SharePoint servers. The folder that contains the feature files is used as the –Path parameter with the Install-SPFeature cmdlet, as shown in Listing 9.17.

LISTING 9.17 **Installing a Feature**

```
Install-SPFeature -Path "CustomSP2013Feature" -Force
```

The –Force switch parameter forces the installation and does not produce any errors if the feature has already been installed.

Uninstalling a Feature

The Uninstall-SPFeature cmdlet allows you to uninstall a feature from SharePoint. Use this in conjunction with the Get-SPFeature cmdlet (explained in a previous section), as shown in Listing 9.18.

LISTING 9.18 **Sample Script for Uninstalling a Feature**

```
$feature = Get-SPFeature

-Identity f3382bc7-93bc-8325-b1c5-7dba9034c7b2

Uninstall-SPFeature $feature  -Force
```

Export Installed Farm Solutions

Using the SharePoint assemblies, you may generate a script that loops through the installed farm solutions and extracts them to a local drive. A sample script is shown in Listing 9.19.

LISTING 9.19 **Sample Script for Exporting All Farm Solutions**

```
[Void][System.Reflection.Assembly]::LoadWithPartialNa
me("Microsoft.SharePoint")

[Void][System.Reflection.Assembly]::LoadWithPartialNa
me("Microsoft.SharePoint.Administration")

$spFarm =

[Micrsoft.SharePoint.Administration.SPFarm]::Local

$spFarmSolutions = $spFarm.Solutions

$localPath = "E:\ExtractedSolutions\"

foreach($spFarmSolution in $spFarmSolutions)

{

[string]$outputFileName =

    $localPath + $spFarmSolution.Name

$spFarmSolution.SolutionFile.SaveAs($outputFileName);

}
```

CHAPTER 10

Configuring and Managing Content Deployment

Creating a New Deployment Path

Creating a new deployment path involves mapping the source web application and site to a target web application and site. You may use the New-SPContentDeploymentPath cmdlet to generate the mapping as shown in Listing 10.1

LISTING 10.1 **Creating a New Content Deployment Path**

```
New-SPContentDeploymentPath
-Name "Sales Internet Content"
-SourceSPWebApplication "SharePoint Root Web"
-SourceSPSite "http://intranet.sp2013.com/Sales"
-DestinationCentralAdministrationURL
     "http://internet.sp2013.com:2345"
-DestinationSPWebApplication
     "SharePointInternetWebApp"
-DestinationSPSite "http://internet.sp2013.com/Sales"
-PathAccount (Get-Credential)
```

Displaying Deployment Paths Configured on the SharePoint 2013 Farm

Use the Get-SPContentDeploymentPath without any parameters as shown in Listing 10.2 to display all available content deployment paths.

LISTING 10.2 **Display All Available Content Deployment Paths**

```
Get-SPContentDeploymentPath
```

110

Retrieving a Specific Content Deployment Path

Providing the identity of the Content Deployment Path with the Get-SPContent DeploymentPath cmdlet, retrieves a specific Content Deployment Path. Use this to assign the results to an object for use in other cmdlets as shown in Listing 10.3.

LISTING 10.3 **Assigning a Variable to a Specific Content Deployment Path**

```
$path = Get-SPContentDeploymentPath
    -Identity "Sales Internet Content"
```

Deleting a Content Deployment Path

The Remove-SPContentDeploymentPath cmdlet allows you to deleye a specific content deployment path configured on the current farm. Simply provide the name of the content deployment path as shown in Listing 10.4

LISTING 10.4 **Remove a Specific Content Deployment Path**

```
Remove-SPContentDeploymentPath "Sales Internet Con-
tent"
```

Creating a New Deployment Job

Creating a new deployment job involves mapping the source web application and site to a target web application and site. You may use the New-SPContentDeploymentJob cmdlet to facilitate this mapping as shown in Listing 10.5

LISTING 10.5 **Creating a New Content Deployment Job**

```
New-SPContentDeploymentJob
      -Name "Sales Deployment Job"
      -SPContentDeploymentPath
            "Sales Internet Content"
```

Displaying Deployment Jobs Configured on the SharePoint 2013 Farm

Using the Get-SPContent Deployment Job without parameters as shown in Listing 10.6 displays all of the deployment jobs.

LISTING 10.6 **Display All Available Content Deployment Jobs**

```
Get-SPContentDeploymentJob
```

Retrieving a Specific Content Deployment Job

Providing the identity of the Content Deployment Job with the Get-SPContent Deployment Job cmdlet, retrieves a specific Content Deployment Job as shown in Listing 10.7.

LISTING 10.7 **Assigning a Variable to a Specific Content Deployment Job**

```
$job = Get-SPContentDeploymentJob
            -Identity "Sales Deployment Job"
```

Deleting a Content Deployment Job

The Remove-SPContentDeploymentJob cmdlet allows you to delete a specific deployment job from the current farm by providing the name of the content deployment job as shown in Listing 10.8

LISTING 10.8 **Remove a Specific Content Deployment Job**

```
Remove-SPContentDeploymentJob "Sales Deployment Job"
```

Starting a Content Deployment Job

The Start-SPContentDeploymentJob cmdlet allows you to manually start a content deployment job by providing the name of the content deployment job as shown in Listing 10.9

LISTING 10.9 **Manually Start a Specific Content Deployment Job**

```
Start-SPContentDeploymentJob "Sales Deployment Job"
```

Modifying Content Deployment Configurations

This chapter covers the basic or more common cmdlets for managing content deployments. For more advance scripting and modifications of content deployment jobs and paths, the following cmdlets are available:

▶ Set-SPContentDeploymentPath

▶ Set-SPContentDeploymentJob

CHAPTER 11

Configuring and Managing User Licensing

This chapter outlines the SharePoint PowerShell commands that are used to manage User Licenses in SharePoint 2013. In previous versions of SharePoint, there was no mechanism to match up user licenses with the SharePoint server licenses. Therefore, users with standard licenses, for example, could still access SharePoint Enterprise features. Using the new SharePoint PowerShell User License cmdlets allows you to enforce user licensing and create appropriate license mappings against security groups.

Displaying User Licensing Status

Use the Get-SPUserLicensing cmdlet without any parameters to retrieve the licensing status.

LISTING 11. 1 **Displaying the Status of User Licensing Enforcement**

```
Get-SPUserLicensing
```

The Get-SPUserLicensing cmdlet displays the current status of user license enforcement and returns an Enabled property as shown in Figure 11.1.

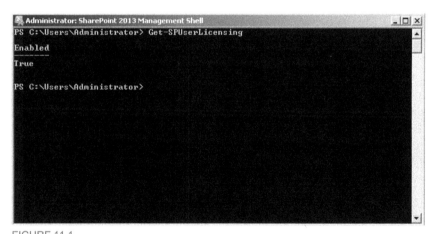

FIGURE 11.1
The Get-SPUserLicensing cmdlet displays the current status

Enabling User Licensing Enforcement

Use the Enable-SPUserLicensing cmdlet without any parameters to enable user licensing.By default, user licensing enforcement is disabled. Using the Enable-SPUserLicensing cmdlet without any parameters, as shown in Listing 11.2, enables the user licensing enforcement within the current SharePoint farm. Use the Get-SPUserLicensing cmdlet as explained in the previous section to verify enablement.

LISTING 8.2 **Enabling the Status of User Licensing Enforcement**

```
Enable-SPUserLicensing
```

Disabling User Licensing Enforcement

Using the Disable-SPUserLicensing cmdlet without any parameters, as shown in Listing 11.3, disables the user licensing enforcement within the current SharePoint farm. Use the Get-SPUserLicensing cmdlet as explained in the previous section to verify disablement.

LISTING 11.3 **Disabling User Licensing Enforcement**

```
Disable-SPUserLicensing
```

Displaying Available User Licenses

Use the Get-SPUserLicense cmdlet without any parameters to retrieve the available user license types.

LISTING 11.4 **Displaying the Available User Licenses**

```
Get- SPUserLicense
```

The Get- SPUserLicense cmdlet displays the available user licenses as shown in Figure 11.2.

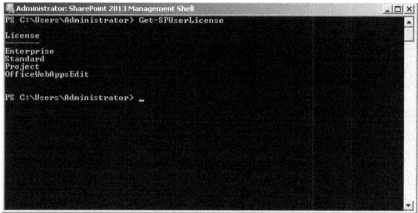

FIGURE 11.2
The Get-SPUserLicensing cmdlet displays the available licenses

118

Creating a New License Mapping

Before you can add a license mapping to user license enforcement, you first need to create a new license mapping object. Use the New-SPUserLicenseMapping cmdlet with the SecurityGroup, Role, ClaimType, or Claim parameters to create a new license mapping. You may assign this to an object variable as shown in Listing 11.5.

LISTING 11.5 **Creating a New License Mapping**

```
$licenseMapping = New-SPUserLicenseMapping -
SecurityGroup "Enterprise Admins" -License Enterprise
```

You may create a mapping against a security group, a forms-based role, a claim type (with the original issuer specified), or a claim itself using the respective parameters. Reviewing the object displays the various properties of the mapping as shown in Figure 11.3.

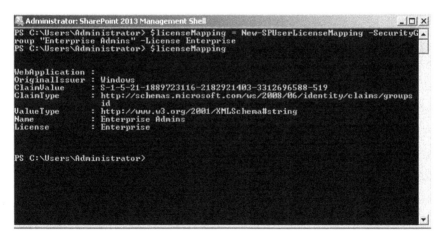

FIGURE 11.3
Viewing a new license mapping object

119

Adding a New License Mapping

Once a new license mapping object is created (as explained in the previous section), you may pass that object variable into the Add-SPUserLicenseMapping cmdlet using the -Mapping parameter as shown in Listing 11.6.

LISTING 11.6 **Adding a New License Mapping**

```
$licenseMapping = New-SPUserLicenseMapping

    -SecurityGroup "Enterprise Admins"

    -License Enterprise

Add-SPUserLicenseMapping -Mapping $licenseMapping
```

Displaying All License Mappings

You may need to see all license mappings that have been created or retrieve the identity of a specific license mapping. Use the Get-SPUserLicenseMapping cmdlet without any parameters as shown in Listing 11.7 to retrieve a listing of all license mappings.

LISTING 11.7 **Displaying All License Mappings**

```
Get-SPUserLicenseMapping
```

Use the optional -WebApplication parameter to only view mappings associated with a particular web application.

Removing a License Mapping

To remove a previously added license mapping, use the Remove-SPUserLicenseMapping cmdlet providing the identity of the license mapping as shown in Listing 11.8.

LISTING 11.8 **Removing a License Mapping**

```
Remove-SPUserLicenseMapping -Identity 3bd51156-49fd-
4122-85d0-58f7019bf270
```

Use the Get-SPUserLicenseMapping cmdlet explained in the previous section to both retrieve the GUID identity of the license mapping you wish to remove as well as verify that the mapping has been removed afterwards.

Service Application Management

CHAPTER 12

Configuring and Managing InfoPath Forms Services

Allowing Browser-Enabled Form Templates

Use the Set-SPInfoPathFormsService cmdlet allow browser enabled forms:

```
Set-SPInfoPathFormsService
-AllowUserFormBrowserEnabling $true
-AllowUserFormBrowserRendering $true
```

Configuring Data Connection Timeouts

Use the Set-SPInfoPathFormsService cmdlet with the data connection timeout parameters. Use the –DefaultDataConnectionTimeout and –MaxDataConnectionTimeout parameters with the Set-SPInfoPathFormsService cmdlet to set the timeout values, as shown in Listing 12.1.

LISTING 12.1 **Data Connection Timeout Cmdlet Line**

```
Set-SPInfoPathFormsService –
DefaultDataConnectionTimeout 15000
–MaxDataConnectionTimeout 25000
```

The timeout values are in milliseconds. The default value for DefaultDataConnectionTimeout is 10000 (10,000 milliseconds, or 10 seconds). The default value for MaxDataConnectionTimeout is 20000 (20,000 milliseconds, 20 seconds).

Configuring Data Connection Response Sizes

Use the MaxDataConnectionResponseSize parameter with the Set-SPInfoPathFormsService cmdlet providing the number of kilobytes the response size should be as shown in Listing 12.2

LISTING 12.2 **Data Connection Response Size Cmdlet Line**

```
Set-SPInfoPathFormsService -
MaxDataConnectionResponseSize 3000
```

Modifying Authentication Settings

Use the Set-SPInfoPathFormsService cmdlet with the appropriate switch parameters to enable or disable data authentication options as shown in Listing 12.3.

LISTING 12.3 **Authentication Settings Configuration Example**

```
Set-SPInfoPathFormsService

    -RequireSslForDataConnections $true

    -AllowEmbeddedSqlForDataConnection $true

    -AllowUdcAuthenticationForDataConnections $true

    -AllowUserFormCrossDomainDataConnections $true
```

Several data authentication options are available that either allow or prohibit certain types of data connectivity:

- **RequireSslForDataConnections**—Set this option to true to require SSL encryption when your form uses HTTP authentication (such as when accessing a web service).

- **AllowEmbeddedSqlForDataConnection**—Set this option to true if you have data connection files that contain SQL database connection information including the username and password.

- **AllowUdcAuthenticationForDataConnections**—Set this option to true to allow custom forms to access data sources through data connection files.

- **AllowUserFormCrossDomainDataConnections**—Select this option if your form needs to access data sources on a different domain than SharePoint.

Configuring Session State

Use the Set-SPInfoPathFormsService cmdlet to configure various session state settings as follows:

- **MaxPostbacksPerSession**—Typically, there shouldn't be too much chatter between the form and Forms Services. This setting prevents unintended postbacks or "out-of-control" communications.

- **MaxUserActionsPerPostback**—There should be only a handful of actions per postback. Once again, this is to prevent a form process from pegging server resources.

- **ActiveSessionTimeout**—By default, active sessions are terminated after 1,440 minutes, which essentially is 24 hours. This is more of a cleanup process than anything. Some forms may take a long time to fill out, depending on the information required, but one day should be plenty of time.

▷ **MaxSizeOfFormSessionState**—This determines how much data can be stored for the active user session. The default is 4,096KB, which equates to 4MB. This provides plenty of room to store user session data. Typical forms and user information should only take up several kilobytes, if not bytes.

LISTING 12.4 **Session State Settings Configuration Example**

```
Set-SPInfoPathFormsService
     -MaxPostbacksPerSession 110
     -ActiveSessionTimeout 720
```

Enabling View State

To enable View State within Form Services in SharePoint 2013, use the AllowViewState parameter with the Set-SPInfoPathFormsService cmdlet. You may also configure the session size using the ViewStateThreshold parameter as shown in Listing 12.5.

LISTING 12.5 **View State Settings Cmdlet Line**

```
Set-SPInfoPathFormsService -AllowViewState $true
-ViewStateThreshold 40961
```

Importing and Exporting Administration Files

You may use the Import-SPInfoPathAdministrationFiles cmdlet to restore a backup file to the InfoPath Forms Services Application in SharePoint 2013 as shown in Listing 12.9.

LISTING 12.9 **Restoring InfoPath Forms Services Files**

```
Import-SPInfoPathAdministrationFiles

    -Path E:\Backups\FormServicesBackup.cab
```

You may use the Export-SPInfoPathAdministrationFiles cmdlet to produce a backup file which contains all of the forms and data connection files that have been deployed to the InfoPath Forms Services Application in SharePoint 2013 as shown in Listing 12.10.

LISTING 12.10 **Backing up InfoPath Forms Services Files**

```
Export-SPInfoPathAdministrationFiles

    -Path E:\Backups\FormServicesBackup.cab
```

CHAPTER 13

Enterprise Search Configuration

Displaying the Enterprise Search Service Information

The Get-SPEnterpriseSearchService cmdlet provides information on the Enterprise Search Service that is running on the SharePoint farm. No parameters are necessary, as shown in Listing 13.1.

LISTING 13.1 **Displaying the Enterprise Search Service Information**

```
Get-SPEnterpriseSearchService
```

The search service information is displayed, as shown in Figure 13.1.

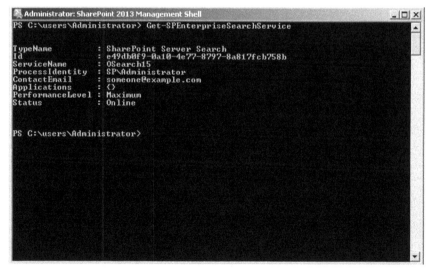

FIGURE 13.1
Displaying the Enterprise Search Service information

132

Displaying Enterprise Search Service Instances

The Get-SPEnterpriseSearchServiceInstance cmdlet provides information on the Enterprise Search Service instances that are mapped to the search service. No parameters are necessary, as shown in Listing 13.2.

LISTING 13.2 **Displaying the Enterprise Search Service Instances**

```
Get-SPEnterpriseSearchServiceInstance
```

The Enterprise Search Service instance information is displayed, as shown in Figure 13.2.

FIGURE 13.2
Displaying the Enterprise Search Service instance information

Retrieving a Specific Enterprise Search Service Instance

Providing the identity of the Enterprise Search Service instance with the Get-SPEnterpriseSearchServiceInstance cmdlet retrieves a specific search service instance. Use this to assign the results to an object for use in other cmdlets, as shown in Listing 13.3.

LISTING 13.3 **Assigning a Variable to a Specific Search Service Application**

```
$ssInstance = Get-SPEnterpriseSearchServiceInstance

-Identity 91d00542-76cf-417b-aafb-dbfae76a1814
```

Configuring the Crawl Account

You may set the crawl account information for the search service by using the CrawlAccount and CrawlPassword parameters with the Set-SPEnterpriseSearchService cmdlet, as shown in Listing 13.4.

LISTING 13.4 **Configuring the Search Service Crawl Account**

```
Set-SPEnterpriseSearchService
-Identity 9e19864d-8b4b-4fda-bcb1-10645457ad70
-CrawlAccount "SP\SharePoint2013CrawlAccount"
-CrawlPassword
(ConvertTo-SecureString -asplaintext -force
 -string "SharePoint2013PWD")
```

The password needs to be a secure string; therefore, the Convert-To-SecureString cmdlet is used to assist. The Crawl Account setting is the Content Access Account when you are managing the Enterprise Search Service on the server.

Configuring the Performance Level

You may set the performance level using the PerformanceLevel parameter with the Set-SPEnterpriseSearchService cmdlet, as shown in Listing 13.5.

LISTING 13.5 **Configuring the Performance Level**

```
Set-SPEnterpriseSearchService

-Identity 9e19864d-8b4b-4fda-bcb1-10645457ad70

-PerformanceLevel Reduced
```

The PerformanceLevel parameter determines how many threads can be utilized by the search service. The valid values are as follows:

- Reduced
- PartlyReduced
- Maximum

The default setting is PartlyReduced.

Displaying the Enterprise Search Service Applications

The Get-SPEnterpriseSearchServiceApplication cmdlet provides information on the Enterprise Search Service applications configured on the current SharePoint 2013 farm. No parameters are necessary, as shown in Listing 13.6.

LISTING 13.6 **Displaying the Enterprise Search Service Applications**

```
Get-SPEnterpriseSearchServiceApplication
```

The Enterprise Search Service application information is displayed, as shown in Figure 13.3.

FIGURE 13.3
Displaying the Enterprise Search Service application information

Retrieving a Specific Enterprise Search Service Application

Providing the identity of the Enterprise Search Service application with the Get-SPEnterpriseSearchServiceApplication cmdlet retrieves a specific Enterprise Search Service application. Use this to assign the results to an object for use in other cmdlets, as shown in Listing 13.7.

LISTING 13.7 **Assigning a Variable to a Specific Search Service Application**

```
$essApp = Get-SPEnterpriseSearchServiceApplication

    -Identity 81aedaf7-704c-47f4-8173-5e99a7495ac3
```

Create a Custom Metadata Category

Creating a metadata category allows you to organize your custom crawled properties. This makes it easier to manage custom search configurations. Creating a new category first allows you to use it when generating your crawled properties.

LISTING 13.8 **Creating a New Metadata Category**

```
$essApp = Get-SPEnterpriseSearchServiceApplication
        -Identity 81aedaf7-704c-47f4-8173-5e99a7495ac3


New-SPEnterpriseSearchMetaDataCategory

    -Name "Custom Property Category"

    -SearchApplication $essApp
```

Several switch parameter options may be used when generating a
new metadata category:

- AutoCreateNewManagedProperties
- DiscoverNewProperties
- MapToContents

Displaying Available Metadata Categories

The Get-SPEnterpriseSearchMetadataCategory cmdlet provides
information on the Enterprise Search metadata categories configured for a particular search service application. Therefore, you
need to provide a search service application with this cmdlet, as
shown in Listing 13.9.

LISTING 13.9 **Displaying the Search Metadata Categories**

```
$essApp = Get-SPEnterpriseSearchServiceApplication
        -Identity 81aedaf7-704c-47f4-8173-5e99a7495ac3


Get-SPEnterpriseSearchMetadataCategory

        -SearchApplication $essApp
```

The Enterprise Search Service metadata categories are displayed,
as shown in Figure 13.4.

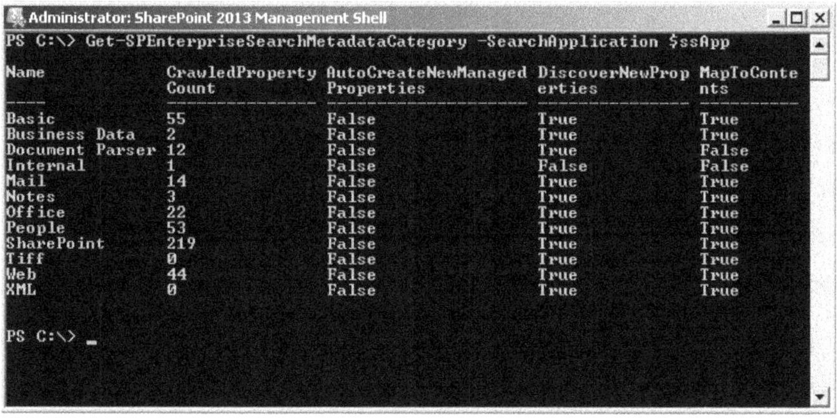

FIGURE 13.4
Displaying the Enterprise Search Service application metadata categories

Retrieving a Specific Metadata Category

Providing the identity of the metadata category with the Get-SPEnterpriseSearchMetadataCategory cmdlet retrieves a specific metadata category for the specified search service application as shown in Listing 13.10.

LISTING 13.10 **Assigning a Variable to a Specific Metadata Category**

```
$essApp = Get-SPEnterpriseSearchServiceApplication
-Identity 81aedaf7-704c-47f4-8173-5e99a7495ac3


$category = Get-SPEnterpriseSearchMetadataCategory

      -SearchApplication $essApp

      -Identity "Custom Property Category"
```

Creating a Custom Metadata Crawled Property

Use the New-SPEneterpriseSearchMetadataCrawledProperty cmdlet to create a new crawled property as shown in Listing 13.11.

LISTING 13.11 **Creating a New Metadata Crawled Property**

```
$essApp = Get-SPEnterpriseSearchServiceApplication
     -Identity 81aedaf7-704c-47f4-8173-5e99a7495ac3

$category = Get-SPEnterpriseSearchMetadataCategory
     -SearchApplication $essApp
     -Identity "SharePoint"

New-SPEnterpriseSearchMetadataCrawledProperty
     -Name "ows_NewField"
     -SearchApplication $essApp
     -Category $category
     -VariantType 31
     -PropSet 00130329-0000-0130-c000-000000131346
     -IsNameEnum $false
```

The VariantType parameter determines the type of data that is stored within the crawled property. The valid types and associated values are as follows:

- Text—31
- Integer—20
- Date and Time—64
- Yes/No—11
- Binary Data—12

PropSet is the property set associated with the category and crawled properties. The best way to find the correct property set is from investigating the crawled properties within Central Administration (from Manage Service Applications, select Search Service Application, select Managed Properties, and then click on Crawled

Properties link at top of screen) or using the Get-SPEnterpriseSearchMetaDataCrawledProperty cmdlet (explained in the next section).

The IsNameEnum switch parameter is required and determines whether the underlying data is actually an integer that is being converted to a string.

Display Available Crawled Properties

The Get-SPEnterpriseSearchMetaDataCrawledProperty cmdlet provides information on the Enterprise Search metadata categories configured for a particular search service application. Therefore, you need to provide a search service application with this cmdlet, as shown in Listing 13.13.

LISTING 13.12 **Displaying the Search Metadata Categories**

```
$essApp = Get-SPEnterpriseSearchServiceApplication
      -Identity 81aedaf7-704c-47f4-8173-5e99a7495ac3
Get-SPEnterpriseSearchMetadataCrawledProperty
      -SearchApplication $essApp
```

The Enterprise Search Service metadata crawled properties are displayed, as shown in Figure 13.5.

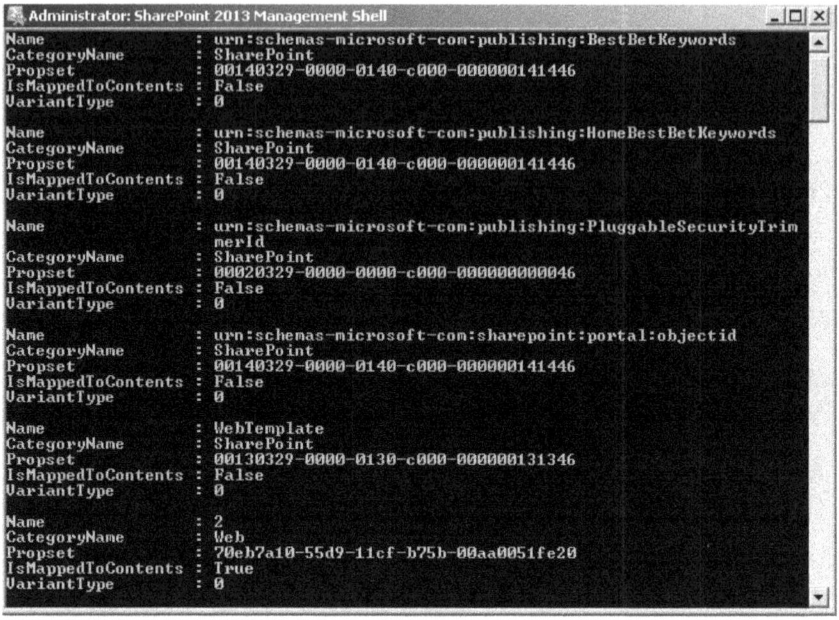

FIGURE 13.5

Displaying the Enterprise Search Service application metadata crawled properties

Get a Specific Metadata Crawled Property

Providing the identity of the metadata crawled property with the Get-SPEnterpriseSearchMetadataCrawledProperty cmdlet retrieves a specific metadata crawled property for the specified search service application. Use this to assign the results to an object for use in other cmdlets, as shown in Listing 13.13.

LISTING 13.13 **Retrieving a Specific Metadata Crawled Property**

```
$essApp = Get-SPEnterpriseSearchServiceApplication
-Identity 81aedaf7-704c-47f4-8173-5e99a7495ac3
$crawledproperty =
    Get-SPEnterpriseSearchMetadataCrawledProperty
        -SearchApplication $essApp
        -Name "ows_NewField"
```

Create a Custom Metadata Managed Property

Instead of crawling content to generate a managed property, you may use this search cmdlet to create a managed property entry within a search service application. This makes it easier when you are replicating search configurations within various environments (development, staging, production, and so on). Sample command lines are shown in Listing 13.14.

LISTING 13.14 **Creating a New Metadata Managed Property**

```
$essApp = Get-SPEnterpriseSearchServiceApplication
      -Identity 81aedaf7-704c-47f4-8173-5e99a7495ac3

$category = Get-SPEnterpriseSearchMetadataCategory
      -SearchApplication $essApp
      -Identity "SharePoint"


New-SPEnterpriseSearchMetadataManagedProperty

      -Name "NewField"

      -SearchApplication $essApp

      -Type 1
```

The Type parameter determines the type of data that is stored within the managed property. The valid types and values are as follows:

- Text—1
- Integer—2
- Decimal—3
- DateTime—4
- YesNo—5
- Binary—6

Display Available Managed Properties

The Get-SPEnterpriseSearchMetadataManagedProperty cmdlet provides information on the Enterprise Search metadata categories configured for a particular search service application. Therefore, you need to provide a search service application with this cmdlet, as shown in Listing 13.15.

LISTING 13.15 **Displaying the Search Metadata Managed Properties**

```
$essApp = Get-SPEnterpriseSearchServiceApplication
      -Identity 81aedaf7-704c-47f4-8173-5e99a7495ac3
Get-SPEnterpriseSearchMetadataManagedProperty
      -SearchApplication $essApp
```

The Enterprise Search Service metadata managed properties are displayed, as shown in Figure 13.6.

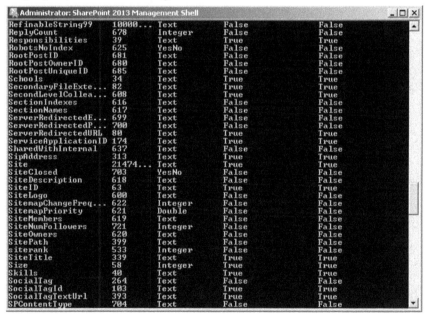

FIGURE 13.6

Displaying the Enterprise Search Service application metadata managed properties

144

Retrieving a Specific Metadata Managed Property

Providing the identity of the metadata managed property with the Get-SPEnterpriseSearchMetadataManagedProperty cmdlet retrieves a specific metadata managed property for the specified search service application. Use this to assign the results to an object for use in other cmdlets, as shown in Listing 13.16.

LISTING 13.16 **Retrieving a Specific Metadata Managed Property**

```
$essApp = Get-SPEnterpriseSearchServiceApplication
-Identity 81aedaf7-704c-47f4-8173-5e99a7495ac3


$managedproperty =

    Get-SPEnterpriseSearchMetadataManagedProperty

    -SearchApplication $essApp

    -Identity NewField
```

Mapping a Crawled Property to a Managed Property

In order to use custom search fields within SharePoint, you must map the crawled properties to managed properties. This is facilitated by suing the New-SPEnterpriseSearchMetadataMapping cmdlet.

LISTING 13.17 **Creating a New Metadata Mapping**

```
$essApp = Get-SPEnterpriseSearchServiceApplication
    -Identity 81aedaf7-704c-47f4-8173-5e99a7495ac3

$crawledproperty =
    Get-SPEnterpriseSearchMetadataCrawledProperty
        -SearchApplication $essApp
        -Name "ows_NewColumn"

$managedproperty =
    Get-SPEnterpriseSearchMetadataManagedProperty
        -SearchApplication $essApp
        -Identity NewColumn


New-SPEnterpriseSearchMetadataMapping

    -SearchApplication $essApp

    -ManagedProperty $managedproperty

    -CrawledProperty $crawledproperty
```

Using Advanced Cmdlets for Search

This chapter covers the basic or more common cmdlets. For more advance scripting with Enterprise Search, Appendix B references all of the search cmdlets.

CHAPTER 14

Configuring and Managing the Profile Service

Retrieving the Identity of the Profile Service Application

In order to get a specific instance of a metadata service application, you need the identity of the service application. The Set-SPProfileServiceApplication cmdlet requires an Identity parameter however there is no Get-SPProfileServiceApplication cmdlet. Therefore, you need to use the Get-SPServiceApplication cmdlet to display all service applications and find the User Profile Service. The command line without any parameters is shown in Listing 14.1.

LISTING 14.1 **Displaying the List of Service Applications**

```
Get-SPServiceApplication
```

Retrieving a Specific Profile Service Application Instance

Providing the identity of the Profile Service Application instance with the Get- SPServiceApplication cmdlet, retrieves a specific secure store service instance. Use this to assign the results to an object for use in other cmdlets as shown in Listing 14.2.

LISTING 14.2 **Retrieving a Specific Metadata Service Application**

```
$profileSA = Get-SPServiceApplication
    -Identity 9b6235e4-f306-4ccc-8192-0c83cb679476
```

Configuring Settings on the Profile Service Application

You may use the Set-SPProfileServiceApplication cmdlet to configure settings on the profile service application using an identity variable as shown in Listing 14.3.

LISTING 14.3 **Configuring the Profile Service Settings**

```
$profileSA = Get-SPServiceApplication
     -Identity 9b6235e4-f306-4ccc-8192-0c83cb679476
Set-SPProfileServiceApplication
     -Identity $profileSA
     -MySiteHostLocation http://sp2013:80/my/
     -MySiteManagedPath my/personal
```

Removing Older Social Items - Comments

The Remove-SPSocialItemByDate allows you to remove comments, tags, or ratings prior to a provided end date. An example command line is shown in Listing 14.4.

LISTING 14.4 **Removing Old Comments from the Profile Service**

```
$profileProxy = Get-SPServiceApplicationProxy
        -Identity 150232e4-a3d2-4915-adb1-155ea77a6dfb
Remove-SPSocialItemByDate
-ProfileServiceApplicationProxy $profileProxy
-RemoveComments:$true
-EndDate 12/1/2013
-Confirm:$false
```

Removing Older Social Items - Ratings

The Remove-SPSocialItemByDate allows you to remove comments, tags, or ratings prior to a provided end date. An example command line is shown in Listing 14.5.

LISTING 14.5 **Removing Old Ratings from the Profile Service**

```
$profileProxy = Get-SPServiceApplicationProxy
        -Identity 150232e4-a3d2-4915-adb1-155ea77a6dfb
Remove-SPSocialItemByDate
        -ProfileServiceApplicationProxy $profileProxy
        -RemoveRatings:$true
        -EndDate 12/1/2013
        -Confirm:$false
```

150

The RemoveRatings is a boolean parameter although it looks like a switch parameter. Therefore either a $true or $false needs to be provided as the boolean value. The service application proxy for the User Profile Service is needed and can be obtained by reviewing the output from Get-SPServiceApplicationProxy.

Removing Older Social Items - Tags

The Remove-SPSocialItemByDate allows you to remove comments, tags, or ratings prior to a provided end date. An example command line is shown in Listing 14.5.

LISTING 14.5 **Removing Old Tags from the Profile Service**

```
$profileProxy = Get-SPServiceApplicationProxy
     -Identity 150232e4-a3d2-4915-adb1-155ea77a6dfb
Remove-SPSocialItemByDate
     -ProfileServiceApplicationProxy $profileProxy
     -RemoveTags:$true
     -EndDate 03/15/2013
     -Confirm:$false
```

Updating the Profile Photo Store

After you upgrade to SharePoint 2013, you need to insure the profile photo store is compatible with SharePoint 2013. Using the Update-SPProfilePhotoStore cmdlet, as shown in Listing 14.6, will insure that the photo store is updated accordingly

LISTING 14.6 **Updating the Profile PhotoStore**

```
Update-SPProfilePhotoStore -MySiteHostLocation
http://mysites
```

Refreshing the Feed Cache

To refresh the feed cache with the last modified times, execute the Update-SPRepopulateMicroblogLMTCache cmdlet using the Profile Service Application Proxy as shown in Listing 14.7.

LISTING 14.7 **Update the Feed Cache**

```
$profileProxy = Get-SPServiceApplicationProxy
     -Identity 150232e4-a3d2-4915-adb1-155ea77a6dfb
Update-SPRepopulateMicroblogLMTCache
     -ProfileServiceApplicationProxy $profileProxy
```

Refreshing a Specific User's Feed Cache

To refresh the feed cache of a specific user, execute the Update-SPRepopulateMicroblogFeedCache using the user's account and the Profile Service Application Proxy as shown in Listing 14.8.

LISTING 14.8 **Update the Feed Cache**

```
$profileProxy = Get-SPServiceApplicationProxy
     -Identity 150232e4-a3d2-4915-adb1-155ea77a6dfb
Update-SPRepopulateMicroblogLMTCache
     -AccountName "SP\FeedUser"
     -ProfileServiceApplicationProxy $profileProxy
```

Using Advanced Cmdlets for the Profile Service

This chapter covers the basic or more common cmdlets for the Profile Service. For more advance scripting, the following cmdlets nouns are also available:

▷ SPSiteSubscriptionProfileConfig

▷ SPProfileServiceApplicationSecurity

▷ SPProfileServiceApplicationProxy

▷ SPProfileLeader

▷ SPProfilePropertyCollection

▷ SPProfileServiceFullReplication

▷ SPProfileServiceRecoveryReplication

▷ SPProfileServiceIncrementalReplication

153

INTENTIONALLY BLANK

CHAPTER 15

Managing and Configuring the Business Data Connectivity Service Application

Retrieving the Identity of the BCS Service Application

In order to get a specific instance of a metadata service application, you need the identity of the service application. The Set-SPBusinessDataCatalogServiceApplication cmdlet requires an Identity parameter however there is no Get-SPBusinessDataCatalogServiceApplication cmdlet.

Therefore, you need to use the Get-SPServiceApplication cmdlet to display all service applications and find the Business Data Connectivity Service. The command line without any parameters is shown in Listing 15.1.

LISTING 15.1 **Displaying the List of Service Applications**

```
Get-SPServiceApplication
```

Retrieving a Specific BCS Service Application Instance

Providing the identity of the Business Data Connectivity Service-Application instance with the Get- SPServiceApplication cmdlet, retrieves a specific Business Data Connectivity Service instance. Use this to assign the results to an object for use in other cmdlets as shown in Listing 15.2.

LISTING 15.2 **Retrieving a Specific a Business Data Service Application**

```
$bcs = Get-SPServiceApplication
     -Identity b7b3652e-6f51-4161-935a-0631a1100ecf
```

156

Configuring the BCS Database

Use the Set-SPBusinessDataCatalogServiceApplication cmdlet with the DatabaseName parameter to configure a new database for BCS in SharePoint 2013 as shown in Listing 15.3.

LISTING 15.3 **Configuring a New Database for BCS**

```
$bcsApp = Get-SPServiceApplication
     -Identity b7b3652e-6f51-4161-935a-0631a1100ecf
Set-SPBusinessDataCatalogServiceApplication
     -Identity $bcsApp
     -DatabaseName BCS_DB
```

Retrieve a BCS Metadata Object

In order to perform import and export operations, you need the related metadata object which stores or will store the BCS entity. Use the Get-SPBusinessDataCatalogMetadataObject cmdlet to set a variable to the metadata object as shown in Listing 15.4.

LISTING 15.4 **Getting a BCS Metadata Object**

```
$bcsMeta =
     Get-SPBusinessDataCatalogMetadataObject
     -ServiceContext http://sp2013
     -BDCObjectType Catalog
     -Name ApplicationRegistry
```

The BDCObjectType may be one of the following values:

- Catalog
- Model
- LobSystem
- LobSystemInstance
- Entity

The Name parameter may be required based on the BDCObjectType that is referenced.

Importing and Exporting BCS Entity Models

The Import-SPBusinessDataCatalogModel allows you to import a model file from a local or shared drive. Use a BCS metadata object variable as the Identity as shown in Listing 15.5.

LISTING 15.5 **Importing a BCS Model**

```
$bcsMeta =
      Get-SPBusinessDataCatalogMetadataObject
      -ServiceContext http://sp2013
      -BDCObjectType Catalog
      -Name ApplicationRegistry

Import-SPBusinessDataCatalogModel
      -Identity $bcsMeta
      -Path F:\DATA\BCS_Model.bdcm
```

The Export-SPBusinessDataCatalogModel allows you to export a model file to a local or shared drive. Use a BCS metadata object variable as the Identity as shown in Listing 15.6.

LISTING 15.6 **Exporting a BCS Model**

```
$bcsMeta =
        Get-SPBusinessDataCatalogMetadataObject
        -ServiceContext http://sp2013
        -BDCObjectType Catalog
        -Name ApplicationRegistry

Export-SPBusinessDataCatalogModel
        -Identity $bcsMeta
        -Path F:\DATA\BCS_Model.bdcm
```

Whether importing or exporting, there are several optional switch parameters that may be used:

- Force – forces an overwrite if the model exists.
- ModelsIncluded – models are included in the imported XML file.
- PermissionsIncluded – the permissions to the model are included.
- PropertiesIncluded – specifies that BCS properties are included.

Setting the Entity Notification Web

The Set-SPBusinessDataCatalogEntityNotificationWeb allows you to specify a Sharepoint web as the entity notification web. Use web object variable or URL for the -Web parameter as shown in Listing 15.7.

LISTING 15.7 **Setting the Entity Notification Web**

```
Set-SPBusinessDataCatalogEntityNotificationWeb
     -Web "http://sp2013"
```

Retrieving the Entity Notification Web

The Get-SPBusinessDataCatalogEntityNotificationWeb retrieves the entity notification web for the provided service context. Use a service context object variable or web application URL for the -ServiceContext parameter as shown in Listing 15.8.

LISTING 15.8 **Getting the Entity Notification Web**

```
Get-SPBusinessDataCatalogEntityNotificationWeb
     -ServiceContext "http://sp2013"
```

Creating an OData Connection

The New-SPODataConnectionSetting allows you to create OData connections for Business Connectivity Services which may be internal or external. An example is shown in Listing 15.9.

LISTING 15.9 **Creating an OData Connection for BCS**

```
New-SPODataConnectionSetting
  -Name "PhillyBikeNetwork"
  -ServiceContext "http://sp2013"
  -ServiceAddressUrl
      "http://gis.phila.gov/ArcGIS/rest/services/Phil
      aOITIS_Transportation/MapServer?f=json&pretty=t
      rue"
-AuthenticationMode Anonymous
```

Successful execution of this cmdlet presents the new OData Connection Settings as shown in Figure 15.1.

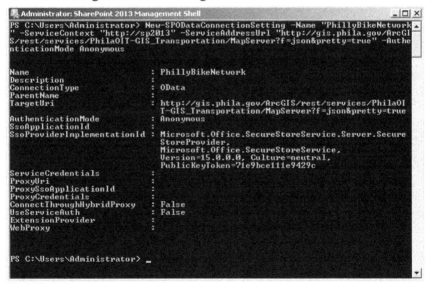

FIGURE 15.1
Creating an OData Connection Setting

161

The AuthenticationMode parameter may be any of the following values:

- Force

- PassThrough

- RevertToSelf

- Credentials

- WindowsCredentials

- DigestCredentials

- ClientCertificate

- Anonymous

If credentials are required, you may set them up using the Secure Store Service and then provide the secure store application ID to the cmdlet using the -SecureStoreTargetApplicationID parameter.

Retrieving an OData Connection

The Get-SPODataConnectionSetting allows you to retrieve OData connection settings. Provide the name of the connection and service context to identity the specific connection. Use a variable to store the settings as shown in Listing 15.10. You may then use the variable in other cmdlets (see next section for an example).

LISTING 15.10 **Getting a Specific OData Connection for BCS**

```
$odata = Get-SPODataConnectionSetting
-Name "PhillyBikeNetwork"
-ServiceContext "http://sp2013"
```

Updating an OData Connection

The Set-SPODataConnectionSetting allows you to update existing OData connections for Business Connectivity Services. You may simply use the Name of the connection as shown in Listing 15.11 or provide an OData Connection setting object using the Identity parameter as shown in Listing 15.12.

LISTING 15.11 **Updating an OData Connection for BCS using the Name**

```
Set-SPODataConnectionSetting
      -Name "PhillyBikeNetwork"
      -ServiceContext "http://sp2013"
       -ServiceAddressUrl
      "http://gis.phila.gov/ArcGIS/rest/services/Phil
      aOITGIS_Transportation/
      MapServer?f=json&pretty=true"
      -AuthenticationMode Anonymous
```

LISTING 15.12 **Updating an OData Connection for BCS using the Identity**

```
$odata = Get-SPODataConnectionSetting
      -Name "PhillyBikeNetwork"
      -ServiceContext "http://sp2013"

Set-SPODataConnectionSetting
      -Identity $odata
      -ServiceContext "http://sp2013"
      -ServiceAddressUrl
      "http://gis.phila.gov/ArcGIS/rest/services/Phil
      aOITGIS_Transportation/
      MapServer?f=json&pretty=true"
      -AuthenticationMode Anonymous
```

If you do not use the -Confim parameter, you are prompted to confirm the update as shown in Figure 15.2.

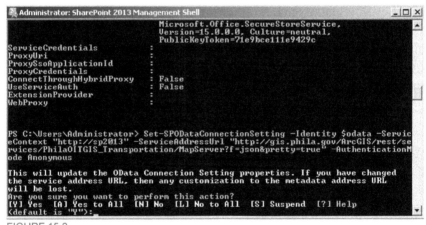

FIGURE 15.2

Updating an OData Connection Setting

CHAPTER 16

Configuring the Secure Store Service Application

Retrieve the Identity of the Secure Store Service Application

In order to get a specific instance of a metadata service application, you need the identity of the service application. The Set-SPSecureStoreServiceApplication cmdlet requires an Identity parameter however there is no Get-SPSecureStoreServiceApplication cmdlet. Therefore, you need to use the Get-SPServiceApplication cmdlet to display all service applications and find the Secure Store Service. The command line without any parameters is shown in Listing 16.1.

LISTING 16.1 **Displaying the List of Service Applications**

```
Get-SPServiceApplication
```

Retrieve a Specific Secure Store Service Application Instance

Providing the identity of the Secure Store Service Application instance with the Get- SPServiceApplication cmdlet, retrieves a specific secure store service instance. Use this to assign the results to an object for use in other cmdlets as shown in Listing 16.2.

LISTING 16.2 **Retrieving a Specific Metadata Service Application**

```
$sss = Get-SPServiceApplication -Identity bc4399ed-
a2e0-4397-bf07-cd3d207e630e
```

Enabling Auditing for the Secure Store Service

There are two audit parameters that may be used with the Set-SPSecureStoreServiceApplication cmdlet. The first parameter, AuditingEnabled, is switch parameter that determines if auditing is enabled. The second parameter, AuditlogMaxSize, determines how many days to retain the logs. Example command lines are shown in Listing 16.3.

LISTING 16.3 **Configuring the Secure Store Service Auditing**

```
$sss = Get-SPServiceApplication
    -Identity bc4399ed-a2e0-4397-bf07-cd3d207e630e
Set-SPSecureStoreServiceApplication
    -Identity $sss
    -AuditingEnabled
    -AuditlogMaxSize 15
```

Configuring the Secure Store Database

Use the Set-SPSecureStoreServiceApplication cmdlet with the DatabaseName parameter to configure a new database for the Secure Store Service application as shown in Listing 16.4.

LISTING 16.4 **Configuring a New Database for the Secure Store Service**

```
$sss = Get-SPServiceApplication
    -Identity bc4399ed-a2e0-4397-bf07-cd3d207e630e
Set-SPSecureStoreServiceApplication
    -Identity $sss
    -DatabaseName SecureStoreDB
```

If the database does not exist, a new database is created.

Generating a New Master Key

The Secure Store Service needs a master key before target applications can be created. To create or change the master key, use the Update-SPSecureStoreMasterKey as shown in Listing 16.5.

LISTING 16.5 **Generating a New Master Key**

```
Update-SPSecureStoreMasterKey
     -ServiceApplicationProxy da9247cb-9055-4024-
     817c-714ef98656e1
     -PassPhrase SharePoint1
```

This cmdlet requires the service application proxy GUID for the Secure Store Service. To find the GUID, use the Get-SPServiceApplicationProxy cmdlet and locate the Secure Store Service entry. The display name cannot be used here. The pass phrase is a plain text entry and does not need to be encrypted.

Refreshing the Encryption Key

After a master key (encryption key) is created or updated, all application servers need to be aware of the key. You may propagate the encryption key to all application servers by using the Update-SPSecureStoreApplicationServerKey cmdlet as shown in Listing 16.6.

LISTING 16.6 **Propogating the Encryption Key to All Application Servers**

```
Update-SPSecureStoreApplicationServerKey
     -ServiceApplicationProxy da9247cb-9055-4024-
     817c-714ef98656e1
     -PassPhrase SharePointPassPhrase
```

This cmdlet requires the service application proxy GUID for the Secure Store Service. To find the GUID, use the Get-SPServiceApplicationProxy cmdlet and locate the Secure Store Service entry. The display name cannot be used here. The pass phrase is a plain text entry and does not need to be encrypted, however, it must match the pass phrase used in the creation of the master key.

Creating Application Fields

When creating a new application for the secure store service, several application fields are needed. These application fields can be created using the New-SPSecureStoreApplicationField cmdlet. The types of fields are as follows:

- Username
- Password
- WindowsUsername
- WindowsPassword
- Key
- Pin
- Generic

Typically you are using the secure store service to provide single-sign-on using a dedicated service account that has access to the application. Therefore, the most common field types are WindowsUsername and WindowsPassword. Use variables to create these fields, as shown in Listing 16.7, such that they may be used when creating a new application entry.

LISTING 16.7 **Creating Application Fields**

```
$windowsUser = New-SPSecureStoreApplicationField
      -Name "SP\AppSvcAccount"
      -Type WindowsUserName
      -Masked:$false


$windowsPass = New-SPSecureStoreApplicationField
      -Name "password"
      -Type WindowsPassword
      -Masked:$true
```

The Masked switch parameter is actually required and therefore must have a $true or $false value. This determines if the field text entry should be masked such as the case with passwords.

When using these fields within other cmdlets, they need to be combined as shown in Listing 16.8.

LISTING 16.8 **Combining Application Fields**

```
$appFields = $windowsUser, $windowsPass
```

Combining the fields produces a fields array as shown in Figure 16.1. This is required by other cmdlets such as New-SPSecureStoreApplication.

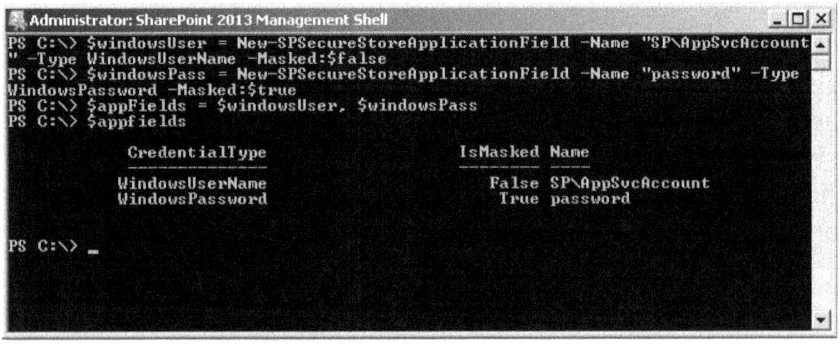

Figure 16.1 Reviewing the Contents of a Fields Array

170

Creating a Target Application

When creating a new application for the secure store service, the target application needs to be specified. The target application object can be created using the New-SPSecureStoreTargetApplication cmdlet. The type of application can be configured using the ApplicationType parameter and one of the following values:

- Individual
- Group
- IndividualWithTicketing
- GroupWithTicketing
- RestrictedIndividual
- RestrictedGroup

Typically you are using the secure store service to provide single-sign-on using a dedicated service account that has access to the application. Therefore, the most common application type is Group. Use a variable to create the target application object, as shown in Listing 16.9, such that the object may be used when creating a new application entry.

LISTING 16.9 **Creating the Target Application**

```
$targetApp = New-SPSecureStoreTargetApplication -Name
"SSOApplication" -FriendlyName "SSO Application" -
ApplicationType Group
```

The Name entry becomes the ApplicationID for the Secure Store Service application and therefore it is recommended to provide a name without spaces. Use the FriendlyName parameter to provide a proper display name.

Creating a New Application Entry

Creating a new application entry essentially combines several of the previous sections into one script such that the New-SPSecureStoreApplication has the necessary values. This involves the target application and application field objects as shown in Listing 16.10.

LISTING 16.10 **Creating the Secure Store Application Entry**

```
$windowsUser = New-SPSecureStoreApplicationField
-Name "SP\AppSvcAccount"
-Type WindowsUserName
-Masked:$false

$windowsPass = New-SPSecureStoreApplicationField
-Name "password"
-Type WindowsPassword
-Masked:$true

$appFields = $windowsUser, $windowsPass

$targetApp = New-SPSecureStoreTargetApplication
-Name "SSOApplication"
-FriendlyName "SSO Application"
-ApplicationType Group

New-SPSecureStoreApplication
-ServiceContext http://sp2013
-TargetApplication $targetApp
-Fields $appFields
```

CHAPTER 17

Configuring the Managed Metadata Service

Retrieving the Identity of the Managed Metadata Service Application

In order to get a specific instance of a metadata service application, you need the identity of the service application. The Get-SPMetadataServiceApplication cmdlet requires an Identity parameter and therefore does not display all instances. Therefore, you need to use the Get-SPServiceApplication cmdlet to display all service applications and find the Managed Metadata Service. The command line without any parameters is shown in Listing 17.1.

LISTING 17.1 **Displaying the List of Service Applications**

```
Get-SPServiceApplication
```

Retrieving a Specific Metadata Service Application Instance

Providing the identity of the Metadata Service Application instance with the Get- SPMetadataServiceApplication cmdlet, retrieves a specific metadata service instance. Use this to assign the results to an object for use in other cmdlets as shown in Listing 17.2.

LISTING 17.2 **Retrieving a Specific Metadata Service Application**

```
$metadataApp = Get-SPMetadataServiceApplication -
Identity f3e6d88a-e0a7-455c-bbef-b4942e7607b5
```

Instead of the GUID, you may use the display name instead. The default display name for the managed metadata service application is "Managed Metadata Service". Since this is a long name, when displaying the service applications, the full text is cut off.

174

Configuring the Metadata Service Accounts

To configure the Managed Metadata Service accounts, use the Set-SPMetadataServiceApplication cmdlet with the account parameters. There are four service account setting parameters for the metadata service application:

- AdministratorAccount
- FullAccessAccount
- RestrictedAccount
- ReadAccessAccount

When setting one of these parameters, the others are removed. Therefore, it is recommended to set all account parameters at the same time as shown in Listing 17.3.

LISTING 17.3 **Configuring the Metadata Service Accounts**

```
Set-SPMetadataServiceApplication

-Identity "Managed Metadata Service"

-AdministratorAccount "SP\Administrator"

-FullAccessAccount "SP\MMDFullAccess"

-RestrictedAccount "SP\MMDRestricted"

-ReadAccessAccount "SP\ReadAccess1,SP\ReadAccess2"
```

You may specify multiple accounts by providing a comma-separated list of the accounts. All accounts specified must exist in the domain.

Configuring the Term Store Database

When the Metadata Service Application is created, by default the database name is Managed Metadata Service_<guid>. You may easily change this to a new database using the DatabaseName parameter with the Set-SPMetadataServiceApplication cmdlet as shown in Listing 17.4.

LISTING 17.4 **Configuring the Term Store Database**

```
Set-SPMetadataServiceApplication -Identity "Managed
Metadata Service" -DatabaseName TermStoreDB
```

If the database does not exist, a new database is created. Simply drop the old one with the GUID in the name and make your DBAs happy. By default the database server is assumed to be the SQL Server instance that SharePoint is using. You may specify the database server by using the –DatabaseServer parameter.

Configuring the Content Type Hub

The content type hub is the site collection you wish to use as your main content type gallery. The metadata service application uses the specified content type hub to consume the content types that exist within the site collection. You may set the content type hub using the HubUri parameter with the Set-SPMetadataServiceApplication cmdlet as shown in Listing 17.5.

LISTING 17.5 **Configuring the Content Type Hub**

```
Set-SPMetadataServiceApplication
      -Identity "Managed Metadata Service"
      -HubUri "http://sp2013"
```

176

Retrieving the Metadata Service Proxy Instances

In order to get a specific instance of a metadata service Application Proxy, you need the identity of the service Application Proxy. The Get-SPMetadataServiceApplicationProxy cmdlet requires an Identity parameter and therefore does not display all instances. Therefore, you need to use the Get-SPServiceApplicationProxy cmdlet to display all service application proxys and find the Managed Metadata Service. The command line without any parameters is shown in Listing 17.6.

LISTING 17.6 **Displaying the List of Service Application Proxys**

```
Get-SPServiceApplicationProxy
```

Retrieving a Specific Metadata Service Application Proxy Instance

Providing the identity of the proxy with the Get- SPMetadataServiceApplicationProxy cmdlet, retrieves a specific Metadata Service Application Proxy instance. Use this to assign the results to an object for use in other cmdlets as shown in Listing 17.7.

LISTING 17.7 **Assigning a Variable to a Specific Metadata Service Proxy**

```
$metadataProxy = Get-SPMetadataServiceApplication
Proxy -Identity f3e6d88a-e0a7-455c-bbef-b4942e7607b5
```

Instead of the GUID, you may use the display name instead. The default display name for the managed metadata service application proxy is "Managed Metadata Service". Since this is a long name, when displaying the service application proxys, the full text is cut off.

Configuring the Managed Metadata Service Connection Options

The metadata service connection settings are configured at the proxy level. Modifying the properties of the metadata service proxy allows for four settings as shown in Figure 17.1.

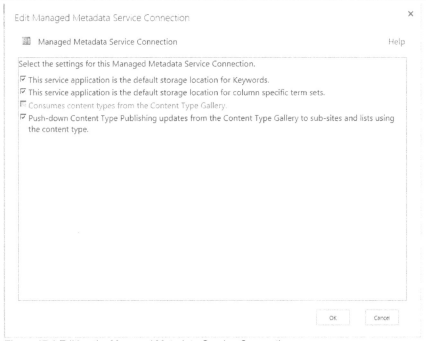

Figure 17.1 Editing the Managed Metadata Service Connection

These four options are synonymous with the following switch parameters of the Set-SPMetadataServiceApplicationProxy cmdlet respectively:

178

- DefaultKeywordTaxonomy
- DefaultSiteCollectionTaxonomy
- ContentTypeSyndicationEnabled
- ContentTypePushdownEnabled

Use the Set-SPMetadataServiceApplicationProxy cmdlet with these switch parameters to configure the Managed Metadata Service connection options as shown in Listing 17.8.

LISTING 17.8 **Configuring the Metadata Service Connection Options**

```
Set-SPMetadataServiceApplicationProxy
  -Identity "Managed Metadata Service"
  -DefaultKeywordTaxonomy
  -DefaultSiteCollectionTaxonomy
  -ContentTypeSyndicationEnabled:$false
  -ContentTypePushdownEnabled:$false
```

CHAPTER 18

Session State and State Service

Enabling and Disabling Session State

To enable session state, execute the Enable-SPSessionStateService cmdlet with the DefaultProvision parameter. This automatically creates the session state database and enables the service using default values. An example command line is shown in Listing 18.1.

LISTING 18.1 **Enabling Session State Using Defaults**

Enable-SPSessionStateService –DefaultProvision

You may alternatively provide the database name and server using the Enable-SPSessionStateService cmdlet as shown in Listing 18.2.

LISTING 18.2 **Enabling Session State with a Specific Database**

Enable-SPSessionStateService –DatabaseName SessionStateDB –DatabaseServer SP2013\SQLSharePoint

Disabling the sessions state can be performed using the Disable-SPSessionStateService cmdlet. Executing this cmdlet will remove the current database and disable the service. An example command line is shown in Listing 18.3.

LISTING 18.3 **Disabling Session State**

Disable-SPSessionStateService

Displaying Session State Information

The Get-SPSessionStateService provides the current information regarding session state within your SharePoint farm. Execute the cmdlet with no parameters as shown in Listing 18.4. If the session state service is enabled, the database information is displayed as shown in Figure 18.1. If the session state service is not enabled, the database information is blank as shown in Figure 18.2 (this is the default after installing a new farm).

LISTING 18.4 **Reviewing the Session State Configuration**

Get-SPSessionStateService

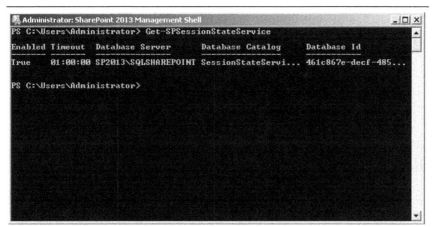

Figure 18.1 Displaying an Enabled Session State Configuration

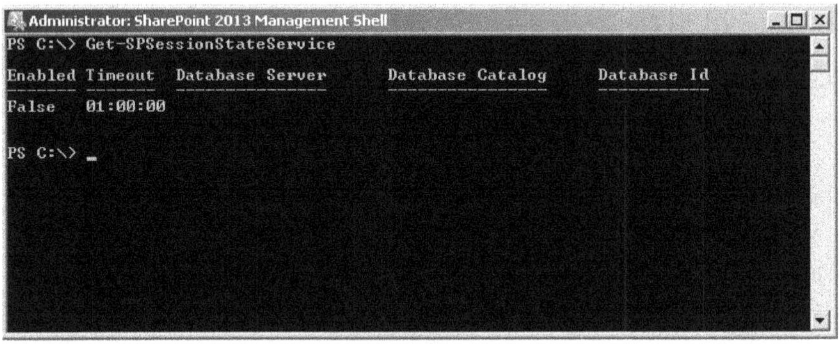

Figure 18.2 Displaying a Disabled Session State Configuration

Configuring the Timeout of the Session State

One of the only configuration changes you may perform on the session state service is changing the timeout value. When viewing the session state configuration (as explained in the previous section) you notice that the timeout is defaulted to one hour (01:00:00). To modify this setting, use the SessionTimeout parameter with the Set-SPSessionStateService as shown in Listing 18.5.

LISTING 18.5 **Decreasing the Session Timeout to 30 Minutes**

```
Set-SPSessionStateService -SessionTimeout 30
```

The SessionTimeout parameter determines the time in minutes when an inactive session should be closed or terminated. While the default is 60 minutes, some organizations may want to be aggressive and use a lower number such as 20 or 30.

Displaying State Service Applications on the SharePoint 2013 Farm

In order to obtain a State Service Application reference object, you need to find the identity of the path entry. Use the Get-SPStateServiceApplication by itself as shown in Listing 18.6 to list out all available State Service Applications.

LISTING 18.6 **Display All Available State Service Applications**

```
Get-SPStateServiceApplication
```

Retrieving a Specific State Service Application

Providing the identity of the State Service Application with the Get-SPStateServiceApplication cmdlet, retrieves a specific State Service Application. Use this to assign the results to an object for use in other cmdlets as shown in Listing 18.7.

LISTING 18.7 **Assigning a Variable to a Specific State Service Application**

```
$stateSA = Get-SPStateServiceApplication -Identity
5da22672-b2ad-4e68-b725-1e91a7e693eb
```

Renaming a State Service Application

You may rename a State Service Application by using the Set-SPStateServiceApplication cmdlet along with the Name parameter. The Identity parameter must be used to identify the state service application that should be modified. An example command line is shown in Listing 18.8.

LISTING 18.8 **Renaming a State Service Application**

```
Set-SPStateServiceApplication -Identity 5da22672-
b2ad-4e68-b725-1e91a7e693eb –Name "State Service App"
```

Performing State Service Database Operations

There are many database operations that may be performed on the state service databases. A listing of available cmdlets can be displayed by issuing the command line shown in Listing 18.9. The result is shown in Figure 18.3.

LISTING 18.9 **Command Line to Display Available Database Operations**

```
SPStateServiceDatabase -?
```

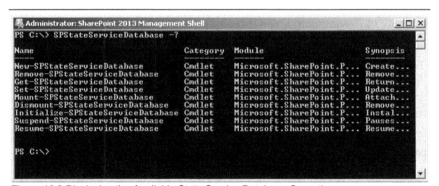

Figure 18.3 Displaying the Available State Service Database Operations

Use any of the provided cmdlets to perform the desired database operation.

CHAPTER 19

Configuring the Work Management Service

Retrieving the Identity of the Work Management Service Application

In order to get a specific instance of a Work Management Service application, you need the identity of the service application. There is no cmdlet to get a work management service application, therefore, you need to use the Get-SPServiceApplication cmdlet to display all service applications and find the Work Management Service. The command line without any parameters is shown in Listing 19.1.

LISTING 19.1 **Displaying the List of Service Applications**

```
Get-SPServiceApplication
```

Retrieving a Specific Work Management Service Application Instance

Providing the identity of the Work Management Service Application instance with the Get- SPServiceApplication cmdlet, retrieves a specific Work Management Service instance. Use this to assign the results to an object for use in other cmdlets as shown in Listing 19.2.

LISTING 19.2 **Assigning a Variable to a Specific Work Management Service Application**

```
$workMgmt = Get-SPServiceApplication
-Identity 61295eb2-c947-4bab-9333-3adee98d9125
```

188

Instead of the GUID, you may use the display name instead. The default display name for the Work Management Service application is "Work Management Service". Since this is a long name, when displaying the service applications, the full text is cut off.

Configuring the Refresh Threshold

You may use the Set-SPWorkManagementServiceApplication cmdlet with the MinimumTimeBetweenProviderRefreshes parameter to configure the minimum amount of time between cache updates. This is on a per user basis. The service application will wait until the time specified before it processes new refresh requests.

The data type of this parameter is System.TimeSpan and therefore it is recommended to create a new timespan variable to provide as shown in Listing 19.3

LISTING 19.3 **Configuring the Refresh Setting**

```
$refreshTimeSpan = New-TimeSpan -Minutes 15

Set-SPWorkManagementServiceApplication
-Identity "Work Management Service"
-MinimumTimeBetweenProviderRefreshes $refreshTimeSpan
```

The Identity parameter may also be a specific Work Management Service application instance using the Get-SPServiceApplication cmdlet as explained in the previous section.

Configuring the Search Query Threshold

You may use the Set-SPWorkManagementServiceApplication cmdlet with the MinimumTimeBetweenSearchQueries parameter to configure the minimum amount of time between calls to the Search Service to identify updated or new tasks within task lists. The search query occurs during the provider refresh process. The service application will wait until the time specified before it processes new search queries.

The data type of this parameter is System.TimeSpan and therefore it is recommended to create a new timespan variable to provide as shown in Listing 19.4

LISTING 19.4 **Configuring the Search Query Setting**

```
$refreshTimeSpan = New-TimeSpan -Minutes 15
Set-SPWorkManagementServiceApplication
-Identity "Work Management Service"
-MinimumTimeBetweenSearchQueries $refreshTimeSpan
```

The Identity parameter may also be a specific Work Management Service application instance using the Get-SPServiceApplication cmdlet as explained in the previous section.

Configuring the User Synchronization Per Server

You may use the Set-SPWorkManagementServiceApplication cmdlet with the -NumberOfExchangeJobsPerServer parameter to configure the maximum amount of users that may be synchronized per server. A server is categorized by any server in the farm that is running the Exchange Server sync timer job.

The data type for this parameter is a System.UInt32 and therefore you may provide an integer value as shown in Listing 19.5. The minimum value technically should be the number of SharePoint users divided by the amount of servers that run timer jobs.

LISTING 19.5 **Configuring the User Synchronization Setting**

```
Set-SPWorkManagementServiceApplication
-Identity "Work Management Service"
-NumberOfExchangeJobsPerServer 1000
```

The actual timer job is named "Work Management Synchronize with Exchange".

Retrieving the Identity of the Work Management Service Proxy

In order to get a specific instance of a Work Management Service Application Proxy, you need the identity of the service Application Proxy. There is no specific cmdlet to get the proxy of a Work Management Service application, therefore, you need to use the Get-SPServiceApplicationProxy cmdlet to display all service application proxys and find the Work Management Service. The command line without any parameters is shown in Listing 19.6.

LISTING 19.6 **Displaying the List of Service Application Proxys**

```
Get-SPServiceApplicationProxy
```

Retrieving a Specific Work Management Service Application Proxy Instance

Providing the identity of the proxy with the Get- SPWorkMan-agementServiceApplicationProxy cmdlet, retrieves a specific Work Management Service Application Proxy instance. Use this to assign the results to an object for use in other cmdlets as shown in Listing 19.7.

LISTING 19.7 **Assigning a Variable to a Specific Work Management Service Proxy**

```
$workMgmtProxy = Get-SPServiceApplicationProxy -
Identity f1e2d3bb-904b-470c-8061-d28e6f411fd7
```

Instead of the GUID, you may use the display name instead. The default display name for the Work Management Service application proxy is "Work Management Service". Since this is a long name, when displaying the service application proxys, the full text is cut off.

CHAPTER 20

Configuring the Machine Translation Service Application

Retrieving the Identity of the Machine Translation Service Application

In order to get a specific instance of a Machine Translation Service application, you need the identity of the service application. There is no cmdlet to get a Machine Translation service application, therefore, you need to use the Get-SPServiceApplication cmdlet to display all service applications and find the Machine Translation Service. The command line without any parameters is shown in Listing 20.1.

LISTING 20.1 **Displaying the List of Service Applications**

```
Get-SPServiceApplication
```

Retrieving a Specific Machine Translation Service Application Instance

Providing the identity of the Machine Translation Service Application instance with the Get- SPServiceApplication cmdlet, retrieves a specific Machine Translation Service instance. Use this to assign the results to an object for use in other cmdlets as shown in Listing 20.2.

LISTING 20.2 **Assigning a Variable to a Specific Machine Translation Service Application**

```
$translation = Get-SPServiceApplication
-Identity 9e5136d3-c1ff-4ef4-b5cd-8fa6c07f027a
```

Instead of the GUID, you may use the display name instead. The default display name for the managed Machine Translation Service application is "Machine Translation Service". Since this is a long

194

name, when displaying the service applications, the full text is cut off.

Retrieving the Identity of the Machine Translation Service Proxy

In order to get a specific instance of a Machine Translation Service Application Proxy, you need the identity of the service Application Proxy. There is no specific cmdlet to get the proxy of a Machine Translation Service application, therefore, you need to use the Get-SPServiceApplicationProxy cmdlet to display all service application proxys and find the Machine Translation Service. The command line without any parameters is shown in Listing 20.6.

LISTING 20.6 **Displaying the List of Service Application Proxys**

```
Get-SPServiceApplicationProxy
```

Retrieving a Specific Machine Translation Service Application Proxy Instance

Providing the identity of the proxy with the Get- SPWorkManagementServiceApplicationProxy cmdlet, retrieves a specific Machine Translation Service Application Proxy instance. Use this to assign the results to an object for use in other cmdlets as shown in Listing 20.7.

LISTING 20.7 **Assigning a Variable to a Specific Machine Translation Service Proxy**

```
$workMgmtProxy = Get-SPServiceApplicationProxy -
Identity f1e2d3bb-904b-470c-8061-d28e6f411fd7
```

Instead of the GUID, you may use the display name instead. The default display name for the managed Machine Translation Service application proxy is "Machine Translation Service". Since this is a long name, when displaying the service application proxys, the full text is cut off.

Configuring the Translation Processes

Use the TotalActiveProcesses parameter with the Set-SPTranslationServiceApplication cmdlet to configure the translation processes. The TotalActiveProcesses parameter determines the how many active translation processes can occur on each server running the Word Services service application. The default is only one process. The valid entries range from 1 to 5 with the default being 1. A sample modification of the active translation processes is shown in Listing 20.8.

LISTING 20.8 **Setting the Total Active Translation Processes**

```
Set-SPTranslationServiceApplication

-Identity "Translation Services" -
TotalActiveProcesses 5
```

The default identity of the Machine Translation Service application is "Translation Services." To find the correct name or GUID, use Get-SPServiceApplication.

Configuring Translations Throughput

Use the TimerJobFrequency and TranslationsPerInstance parameters with the Set-SPTranslationServiceApplication cmdlet to condifure the translations throughput.The translation throughput parameters TimerJobFrequency and TranslationsPerInstance correspond to the Machine Translation Services configuration settings, as shown in Figure 20.1.

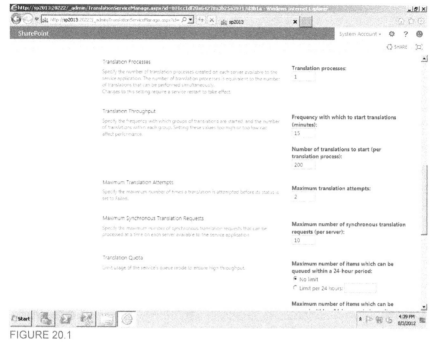

FIGURE 20.1

Translation throughput configuration settings in Central Administration

To get to these properties, from Central Admin, click on the Manage Service Applications link under Application Management. Locate the Machine Translation Services entry and highlight the connection and then click on the Properties button from the top ribbon bar.

The TimerJobFrequency parameter determines how often the translation process should be started using the corresponding service timer job. The default is 15 minutes, and the valid range maybe any number of minutes between 1 and 59.

The TranslationsPerInstance parameter determines how many Translations may be processed per instance. The default value is 300 translations.

A sample command line for setting the translation throughput values is shown in Listing 20.9.

LISTING 20.9 **Setting the Translation Throughput Values**

```
Set-SPTranslationServiceApplication

-Identity "Machine Translation Services"

-TimerJobFrequency 5 -TranslationsPerInstance 100
```

The values for throughput should be modified based on usage of Machine Translation Services within your organization. Heavy usage may warrant more frequent timer job execution. Increasing the amount of minutes for the timer job may warrant an increase in Translations per instance; however, increasing these values could cause performance issues. Use these values along with the active processes to balance the usage and optimize throughput.

Configuring Enabled Document File extensions for Translation

Use the AddEnabledFileExtensions and RemoveEnabledFileExtensions parameters with the Set-SPTranslationServiceApplication cmdlet to configure the enabled document file extensions used for translation.

By default, all available document file extensions are supported within Machine Translation Services. You may use the AddEnabledFileExtensions or RemoveEnabledFileExtensions parameter with the Set-SPTranslationServiceApplication cmdlet to modify which set of file extensions is enabled.

Both of these parameters take a comma-separated list of valid document file extensions. The recognized values are as follows:

- **docx**
- **doc**
- **docm**
- **dotx**
- **dotm**
- **dot**
- **rtf**
- **html**
- **htm**
- **aspx**
- **xhtml**
- **xhtm**
- **txt**
- **xlf**

These file extensions correspond to the available options available through Central Administration, as shown in Figure 20.2. Sample command lines are shown in Listing 20.10.

LISTING 20.10 **Modifying the Enabled File Extensions**

```
Set-SPTranslationServiceApplication
          -Identity "Machine Translation Services"
          -RemoveEnabledFileExtensions rtf,mht


Set-SPTranslationServiceApplication

-Identity "Machine Translation Services" -
AddEnabledFileExtensions docx,doc
```

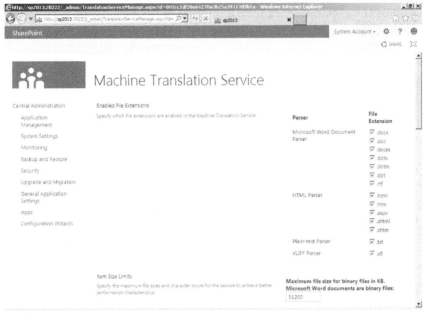

FIGURE 20.2
Supported document extensions for Machine Translation Services

You may use quotes around a single file format; however, when you are providing a comma-separated list of file extensions, quotes cannot be used. No errors will be presented, although the operation will not modify the settings.

Modifying Database Information

Use the database parameters with the Set-SPTranslationServiceApplication cmdlet to configure the database settings.Three database parameters may be used to configure the database settings for Word Services: DatabaseServer, Database-Name, and DatabaseCredential.

The DatabaseCredential parameter is only used if the authorization is performed through SQL Authentication. Even though all of these parameters are optional overall, if the DatabaseCredential parameter is used, then the DatabaseServer and DatabaseName become

200

required. A sample modification of the database settings is shown in Listing 20.11.

LISTING 20.11 **Changing the Database Configuration for Translation Services**

```
$trans = Get-SPServiceApplication
-Identity 9e5136d3-c1ff-4ef4-b5cd-8fa6c07f027a
Set-SPTranslationServiceApplication -Identity $trans
      -DatabaseServer SP2013

      -DatabaseName SP2013TranslationServices

      -DatabaseCredential (Get-Credential)
```

If the database that is described within the DatabaseName parameter does not exist, it will be created automatically

Modifying Translation Timeouts

Use the KeepAliveTimeout or MaximumTranslationTime parameter with the Set-SPTranslationServiceApplication cmdlet to configure translation timeout settings.

Provide the KeepAliveTimeout parameter to determine how many seconds a process can be nonresponsive before it is terminated. The valid values for this setting are from 60 to 600 seconds and the default is 60 seconds.

Provide the MaximumTranslationTime parameter to determine how long a translation should continue running. The default is 600 seconds, whereas the valid range is 600-3600 seconds. A sample modification of the translation timeout setting is shown in Listing 20.12.

LISTING 20.12 **Changing the Translation Timeout Settings**

```
Set-SPTranslationServiceApplication -Identity "Ma-
chine Translation Services" -KeepAliveTimeout 120 -
MaximumTranslationTime 1200
```

Modifying the Maximum Translation Attempts

Use the MaximumTranslationAttempts parameter with the Set-SPTranslationServiceApplication cmdlet to configure how many attempts should be taken before a translation is considered a failure. The default is 2 (attempts) and the range of valid values is 1 to 10. A sample modification of the maximum translation attempts setting is shown in Listing 20.13.

LISTING 20.13 **Changing the Maximum Translation Attempts Setting**

```
Set-SPTranslationServiceApplication

    -Identity "Machine Translation Services"

    -MaximumTranslationAttempts 3
```

The default is two attempts but three seems like a normal setting. Anything more than five is probably too optimistic. If the translation fails after three times, there is a 90% chance it will continue to fail

.

Modifying the Recycle Threshold

Use the RecycleProcessThreshold parameter with the Set-SPTranslationServiceApplication cmdlet to configure the recycle threshold setting. The RecycleProcessThreshold parameter allows you to specify the number of documents each translation process can convert before the process is recycled. The default value is 100 (documents), whereas the valid range of values is 1 to 1000. A sample threshold modification is shown in Listing 20.14.

LISTING 20.14 **Changing the Recycle Threshold**

```
Set-SPTranslationServiceApplication
      -Identity "Machine Translation Services"
      -RecycleProcessThreshold 200
```

Microsoft Office

CHAPTER 21

Managing and Configuring Excel Services

Create a Trusted File Location

The New-SPExcelFileLocation cmdlet may be used to create a new trusted location to access Excel workbooks. Provide the address of the location and the Excel Services Application instance, as shown in Listing 21.1.

LISTING 21.1 **Creating a New Trusted File Location**

```
New-SPExcelFileLocation
      -Address "http://sp2013/Excel Workbooks"
      -ExcelServiceApplication "Excel Services
Application"
      -LocationType SharePoint
      -IncludeChildren
```

The –LocationType parameter may be one of the following:

- SharePoint (default)
- UNC
- HTTP

The –IncludeChildren switch parameter is used to specify that any folders or locations underneath the address should also be trusted.

Upon successful creation of the new trusted file location, a summary of the properties is displayed, as shown in Figure 21.1.

FIGURE 21.1

Creating a new trusted file location

Displaying All Trusted File Locations

Using the Get-SPExcelFileLocation cmdlet with the ExcelSer-viceApplication parameter as shown in Listing 21.2 displays all configured trusted file locations, as shown in Figure 21.2.

LISTING 21.2 **Displaying All Trusted File Locations**

```
Get-SPExcelFileLocation
      -ExcelServiceApplication "Excel Services
      Application"
```

```
Administrator: SharePoint 2013 Management Shell                              _ |□| x|
PS C:\> Get-SPExcelFileLocation -ExcelServiceApplication "Excel Services Applica
tion"

Address                                    : http://
Identity                                   : http://
LocationType                               : SharePoint
IncludeChildren                            : True
SessionTimeout                             : 450
ShortSessionTimeout                        : 450
NewWorkbookSessionTimeout                  : 1800
RequestDurationMax                         : 300
ChartRenderDurationMax                     : 3
WorkbookSizeMax                            : 10
ChartAndImageSizeMax                       : 1
AutomaticVolatileFunctionCacheLifetime     : 300
DefaultWorkbookCalcMode                    : File
ExternalDataAllowed                        : DclAndEmbedded
WarnOnDataRefresh                          : True
DisplayGranularExtDataErrors               : True
AbortOnRefreshOnOpenFail                   : True
PeriodicExtDataCacheLifetime               : 300
ManualExtDataCacheLifetime                 : 300
ConcurrentDataRequestsPerSessionMax        : 5
UdfsAllowed                                : True
Description                                :
RESTExternalDataAllowed                    : False
ExcelServiceApplication                    : Excel Services Application

Address                                    : http://sp2013/Excel Workbooks
Identity                                   : http://sp2013/Excel Workbooks
LocationType                               : SharePoint
IncludeChildren                            : True
SessionTimeout                             : 450
ShortSessionTimeout                        : 450
NewWorkbookSessionTimeout                  : 1800
RequestDurationMax                         : 300
ChartRenderDurationMax                     : 3
WorkbookSizeMax                            : 10
ChartAndImageSizeMax                       : 1
AutomaticVolatileFunctionCacheLifetime     : 300
DefaultWorkbookCalcMode                    : File
ExternalDataAllowed                        : DclAndEmbedded
WarnOnDataRefresh                          : True
DisplayGranularExtDataErrors               : True
AbortOnRefreshOnOpenFail                   : True
PeriodicExtDataCacheLifetime               : 300
ManualExtDataCacheLifetime                 : 300
ConcurrentDataRequestsPerSessionMax        : 5
UdfsAllowed                                : False
Description                                :
RESTExternalDataAllowed                    : False
ExcelServiceApplication                    : Excel Services Application
```

FIGURE 21.2

The Get-SPExcelFileLocation cmdlet displays all trusted file locations.

Retrieving a Specific Trusted File Location

Providing the identity of the trusted file location to the Get-SPExcelFileLocation cmdlet retrieves a specific trusted file location instance. Use this to assign the results to a variable for use in other cmdlets, as shown in Listing 21.3.

LISTING 21.3 **Assigning a Variable to a Specific Trusted File Location**

```
$trustedLocation = Get-SPExcelFileLocation
-Identity "http://sp2013/Excel Workbooks"
-ExcelServiceApplication "Excel Services Application"
```

Removing a Trusted File Location

The Remove-SPExcelFileLocation cmdlet allows you to remove a
specific trusted file location from Excel Services. Use this in conjunction with the Get-SPExcelFileLocation cmdlet (explained in a
previous section), as shown in Listing 21.4.

LISTING 21.4 **Sample Script for Removing a Trusted File Location**

```
$trustedLocation = Get-SPExcelFileLocation
      -Identity "http://sp2013/Excel Workbooks"
      -ExcelServiceApplication "Excel Services
      Application"

Remove-SPExcelFileLocation $trustedLocation
-ExcelServiceApplication "Excel Service Application"
```

Creating a Trusted Data Connection Library

The New-SPExcelDataConnectionLibrary cmdlet may be used to
create a new trusted data connection location that Excel workbooks
can access. Provide the address of the data connection library and
the Excel Services Application instance, as shown in Listing 21.5.

212

LISTING 21.5 **Creating a New Trusted Data Connection Library**

```
New-SPExcelDataConnectionLibrary
    -Address "http://sp2013/Data Connections"
    -ExcelServiceApplication "Excel Services
    Application"
```

Upon successful creation of the new trusted data connection library, a summary of the properties is displayed, as shown in Figure 21.3.

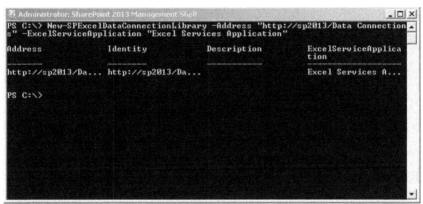

FIGURE 21.3
Creating a new data connection library entry.

Displaying All Trusted Data Connection Libraries

Using the Get-SPExcelDataConnectionLibrary cmdlet with the ExcelServiceApplication parameter, as shown in Listing 21.6, displays all configured trusted data connection libraries.

LISTING 21.6 **Displaying All Trusted Data Connection Libraries**

```
Get-SPExcelDataConnectionLibrary
-ExcelServiceApplication "Excel Services Application"
```

Retrieving a Specific Trusted Data Connection Library

Use the Get-SPExcelDataConnectionLibrary cmdlet to assign a variable the results using the –Identity and –ExcelServiceApplication parameters to retrieve specific trusted data connection library.

Providing the identity of the trusted data connection library to the Get-SPExcelDataConnectionLibrary cmdlet retrieves a specific data connection library instance. Use this to assign the results to a variable for use in other cmdlets, as shown in Listing 21.7.

LISTING 21.7 **Assigning a Variable to a Specific Data Connection Library**

```
$trustedLibrary = Get-SPExcelDataConnectionLibrary
     -Identity "http://sp2013/Data Connections"
     -ExcelServiceApplication "Excel Services
     Application"
```

Removing a Trusted Data Connection Library

The Remove-SPExcelDataConnectionLibrary cmdlet allows you to remove a specific trusted data connection library from Excel Services. Use this in conjunction with the Get-SPExcelDataConnectionLibrary cmdlet (explained in a previous section), as shown in Listing 21.8.

LISTING 21.8 **Removing a Trusted Data Connection Library**

```
$trustedLibrary =
     Get-SPExcelDataConnectionLibrary
     -Identity "http://sp2013/Data
     Connections"
     -ExcelServiceApplication "Excel Services
     Application"

Remove-SPExcelDataConnectionLibrary $trustedLibrary
     -ExcelServiceApplication "Excel Service
     Application"
```

Creating a New Safe Data Provider

The New-SPExcelDataProvider cmdlet may be used to create a new safe data provider that Excel workbooks can access via a data connection. Provide the provider information and the Excel Services Application instance, as shown in Listing 21.9.

LISTING 21.9 **Creating a New Safe Data Provider**

```
New-SPExcelDataProvider

-ExcelServiceApplication "Excel Services Application"

-ProviderID "Custom DB"

-ProviderType ODBC
```

The –ProviderID is an identifier for the data provider. The –ProviderType can be any of the following values:

- OLEDB
- ODBC
- ODBCDSN

Upon successful creation of the new safe data provider, a summary of the properties is displayed, as shown in Figure 21.4.

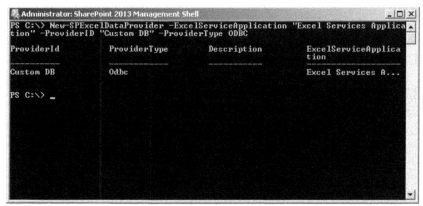

FIGURE 21.4
Creating a new data provider entry

Displaying All Safe Data Providers

Using the Get-SPExcelDataProvider cmdlet with the ExcelServiceApplication parameter, as shown in Listing 21.10, displays all configured trusted data connection libraries.

LISTING 21.10 **Displaying All Trusted Data Connection Libraries**

```
Get-SPExcelDataProvider

-ExcelServiceApplication "Excel Services Application"
```

Retrieving a Specific Safe Data Provider

The Get-SPExcelDataProvider cmdlet does not have an Identity or ProviderID parameter and therefore only returns the entire list of safe data providers. Therefore, you need to pipe the output to a where clause that finds the particular data provider based on the provider ID. In order to accomplish this filtering while providing the required Excel Service Application object, you first need to pipe the Excel Service Application object into the Get-SPExcelDataProvider cmdlet.

This sounds more complicated than it actually is implemented. An example is shown in Listing 21.11.

LISTING 21.11 **Assigning a Variable to a Specific Data Provider**

```
$dataProvider = Get-SPExcelServiceApplication

-Identity "Excel Services Application"

| Get-SPExcelDataProvider

 | where {$_.ProviderID -eq "Custom DB"}
```

Removing a Safe Data Provider

The Remove-SPExcelDataProvider cmdlet allows you to remove a specific safe data provider from Excel Services. Use this in conjunction with the Get-SPExcelDataProvider cmdlet (explained in a previous section), as shown in Listing 21.12.

LISTING 21.12 **Removing a Safe Data Provider**

```
$dataProvider = Get-SPExcelServiceApplication
-Identity "Excel Services Application"
| Get-SPExcelDataProvider
 | where {$_.ProviderID -eq "Custom DB"}

Remove-SPExcelDataProvider $dataProvider
```

The Remove-SPExcelDataProvider cmdlet doesn't require an Excel Service Application parameter, which makes up for the trouble of having to generate the proper data provider object.

Creating a Blocked File Type

The New-SPExcelBlockedFileType cmdlet may be used to block a specific type of Excel workbook from Excel Services. Provide the file type and the Excel Services Application instance, as shown in Listing 21.13.

LISTING 21.13 **Creating a New Blocked File Type**

```
New-SPExcelBlockedFileType

-ExcelServiceApplication "Excel Services Application"
-FileType XLSB
```

The –FileType can be one of the following:

- XLSX
- XLSM
- XLSB

Essentially you are blocking Excel 2010 Workbooks, Macro-Enabled Workbooks, or Binary-Enabled Workbooks (or some combination thereof).

Displaying All Blocked File Types

Using the Get-SPExcelBlockedFileType cmdlet with the ExcelServiceApplication parameter, as shown in Listing 21.14, displays all configured blocked file types.

LISTING 21.14 **Displaying All Blocked File Types**

```
Get-SPExcelBlockedFileType

-ExcelServiceApplication "Excel Services Application"
```

Retrieving a Specific Blocked File Type

Providing the identity of the blocked file type to the Get-
SPExcelBlockedFileType cmdlet retrieves a specific blocked file
type instance. Use this to assign the results to a variable for use in
other cmdlets, as shown in Listing 21.15.

LISTING 21.15 **Assigning a Variable to a Specific Blocked File Type**

```
$blockedFileType = Get-SPExcelBlockedFileType

-Identity "XLSB"

-ExcelServiceApplication "Excel Services Application"
```

Removing a Blocked File Type

The Remove-SPExcelBlockedFileType cmdlet allows you to remove a specific blocked file type from Excel Services. Use this in
conjunction with the Get-SPExcelBlockedFileType cmdlet (explained in a previous section), as shown in Listing 21.16.

LISTING 21.16 **Removing a Blocked File Type**

```
$blockedFileType =

    Get-SPExcelBlockedFileType -Identity "XLSB"
        -ExcelServiceApplication "Excel Services
        Application"

Remove-SPExcelBlockedFileType $blockedFileType
    -ExcelServiceApplication "Excel Service
    Application"
```

Create a User-Defined Function Reference

The New-SPExcelUserDefinedFunction cmdlet may be used to create a reference to an assembly that can be used to call user-defined functions within Excel workbooks running under Excel Services. Provide the assembly information and the Excel Services Application instance, as shown in Listing 21.17.

LISTING 21.17 **Creating a New User-Defined Function Reference**

```
New-SPExcelUserDefinedFunction
-ExcelServiceApplication "Excel Services Application"
-Assembly "MyCompany.ExcelServices.UDF,
      Version=1.0.0.0, Culture=neutral,
      PublicKeyToken=82e6dce111e9429c"
-AssemblyLocation GAC
```

The –AssemblyLocation can be one of the following:

- GAC
- LocalFile

For security as well as central access, user-defined functions should be compiled into a DLL and placed in the GAC.

Modifying Excel Services Objects

This chapter covers the basic or more common cmdlets for creating and using Excel Services objects. For more advance scripting and modifications of these objects, the following cmdlets are available:

- Set-SPExcelServicesApplication
- Set-SPExcelDataConnectionLibrary
- Set-SPExcelDataProvider

- Set-SPExcelFileLocation
- Set-SPExcelUserDefinedFunction

CHAPTER 22

PerformancePoint Services

Configuring the Unattended Service Account

In order to use PerformancePoint Services (PPS) within SharePoint 2013 you need to set the unattended service account. This account is used to access the data sources for PPS. This may be facilitated using the Set-SPPerformancePointSecureDataValues cmdlet as shown in Listing 22.1.

LISTING 22.1 **Setting the Unattended Service Account**

```
Set-SPPerformancePointSecureDataValues -
ServiceApplication "PerformancePoint Service Applica-
tion" -DataSourceUnattendedServiceAccount (Get-
Credential)
```

The default PerformancePoint Services Application is named "PerformancePoint Service Application". To find the correct name or GUID, use Get-SPServiceApplication or Get-SPPerformancePointServiceApplication.

Displaying the Unattended Service Account

To display the unattended service account that is configured for PPS data sources, use the Get-SPPerformancePointSecureValues cmdlet with the -ServiceApplication parameter as shown in Listing 22.2.

LISTING 22.2 **Displaying the Unattended Service Account**

```
Get-SPPerformancePointSecureDataValues -
ServiceApplication "PerformancePoint Service Applica-
tion"
```

The account name will be displayed but not the password. The default PerformancePoint Services Application is named "PerformancePoint Service Application". To find the correct name or GUID, use Get-SPServiceApplication or Get-SPPerformancePointServiceApplication.

Creating a Trusted Content Location

The New-SPPerformancePointServiceApplicationTrustedLocation may be used to create a new trusted content location to access PPS content. Provide the address (URL) of the location, type, and the PerformancePoint Services Application instance as shown in Listing 22.2.

LISTING 22.2 **Create a New Trusted Content Location**

```
New-
SPPerformancePointServiceApplicationTrustedLocation -
Url "http://sp2013/Lists/PPS Content" -
ServiceApplication "PerformancePoint Service Applica-
tion" -Type List -TrustedLocationType Content
```

The –Type may be one of the following when creating a content location:

- ▶ SiteCollection
- ▶ Site
- ▶ List

Passing in "Content" with the –TrustedLocationType parameter determines that this location is a content location for PPS. Although DocumentLibrary is a valid –Type, it is not valid for content locations.

Creating a Trusted Data Source Location

The New-SPPerformancePointServiceApplicationTrustedLocation may be used to create a new trusted data source location such a that PPS may access data connections . Provide the address (URL) of the location, type, and the PerformancePoint Services Application instance as shown in Listing 22.2.

LISTING 22.3 **Create a New Trusted Data Source Location**

```
New-
SPPerformancePointServiceApplicationTrustedLocation
-Url "http://sp2013/PPS DataSource"
-ServiceApplication
     "PerformancePoint Service Application"
-Type DocumentLibary
-TrustedLocationType DataSource
```

The –Type may be one of the following when creating a content location:

- SiteCollection
- Site
- DocumentLibrary

Passing in "DataSource" with the –TrustedLocationType parameter determines that this location is a data source location for PPS. Although List is a valid –Type, it is not valid for data source locations.

Displaying All Trusted Content Locations

In order to filter the list of trusted locations you need to use a piped where clause with the Get-SPPerformancePointServiceApplicationTrustedLocation cmdlet. Since this cmdlet doesn't show detailed information by default, the –Identity parameter must be used. The service application is therefore piped into this cmdlet. An example command line is shown in Listing 22.4

LISTING 22.4 **Display All Trusted Content Locations**

```
Get-SPPerformancePointServiceApplication "Performance
Point Service Application" | Get-
SPPerformancePointServiceApplicationTrustedLocation -
Identity $_.ID | where {$_.FileType -eq "Content"}
```

Displaying All Trusted DataSource Locations

In order to filter the list of trusted locations you need to use a piped where clause with the Get-SPPerformancePointServiceApplicationTrustedLocation cmdlet. Since this cmdlet doesn't show detailed information by default, the –Identity parameter must be used. The service application is therefore piped into this cmdlet. An example command line is shown in Listing 22.5

LISTING 22.5 **Displaying All Trusted DataSource Locations**

```
Get-SPPerformancePointServiceApplication "Performance
Point Service Application" | Get-
SPPerformancePointServiceApplicationTrustedLocation -
Identity $_.ID | where {$_.FileType -eq "DataSource"}
```

227

Displaying Details of Trusted Locations

To view all the details of the trusted locations, such as the identity GUID, you need to use the –Identity parameter with Get-SPPerformancePointServiceApplication while piping the results to a "select *" directive. The service application needs to be piped into the Get-SPPerformancePointServiceApplication cmdlet as shown in Listing 22.6

LISTING 22.6 **Displaying All Details of the Trusted Locations**

```
Get-SPPerformancePointServiceApplication "Performance
Point Service Application" | Get-
SPPerformancePointServiceApplicationTrustedLocation -
Identity $_.ID | select *
```

Once the details are displayed, you may fine tune your select directive to only retrieve the information you need (e.g. select url, id).

Retrieving a Specific Trusted Location

Providing the identity of the trusted data connection library to the Get-SPPerformancePointServiceApplicationTrustedLocation cmdlet retrieves a specific data connection library instance. Use this to assign the results to a variable for use in other cmdlets as shown in Listing 22.7.

LISTING 22.7 **Assigning a Variable to a Specific Trusted Location**

```
$trustedLocation = Get-
SPPerformancePointServiceApplicationTrustedLocation -
Identity fab6396b-5cd3-4f17-be60-57ae7d18c8a6
```

Removing a Trusted Location

The Remove-SPPerformancePointServiceApplicationTrustedLocation cmdlet allows you to remove a specific trusted location from PerformancePoint Services. Use this in conjunction with the Get-SPPerformancePointServiceApplicationTrustedLocation cmdlet (explained in the previous section) as shown in Listing 22.8.

LISTING 22.8 **Example Script for Removing a Trusted Location**

```
$trustedLocation = Get-
SPPerformancePointServiceApplicationTrustedLocation -
Identity fab6396b-5cd3-4f17-be60-57ae7d18c8a6

Remove-
SPPerformancePointServiceApplicationTrustedLocation
$trustedLocation
```

Configuring Enforcement of Trusted Locations

By default, all SharePoint locations are trusted as for content and data sources. Even if you added new locations using the cmdlets in the previous sections, they will be added but not enforced.

To restrict PerformancePoint Services to only use the configured trusted locations, use the Set-SPPerformancePointServiceApplication cmdlet with the trusted location parameters as shown in Listing 22.9 and Listing 22.10.

LISTING 22.9 **Enforce Trusted Content Locations**

```
Set-SPPerformancePointServiceApplication -Identity
"PerformancePoint Service Application" -
TrustedContentLocationsRestricted $true
```

LISTING 22.10 **Enforce Trusted Data Source Locations**

```
Set-SPPerformancePointServiceApplication -Identity
"PerformancePoint Service Application" -
TrustedDataSourceLocationsRestricted $true
```

Use $false to disable the enforcement of the trusted locations and allow all SharePoint locations to be acceptable.

Configuring Application Settings

The Set-SPPerformancePointServiceApplication cmdlet allows you to configure various settings within the PerformancePoint Service Application specified. Pass in the name or the ID of the service application instance using the –Identity parameter and use one or more of the optional parameters to modify the appropriate settings. An example modification of the PerformancePoint Service Application settings is shown in Listing 22.11

LISTING 22.11 **Modifying the Application Settings**

```
Set-SPPerformancePointServiceApplication -Identity
"PerformancePoint Service Application" -
CommentsDisabled $false -CommentsScorecardMax 100
```

CHAPTER 23

Access Services

Configuring the Application Log Size

Use the ApplicationLogSize parameter with the Set-SPAccessServiceApplication cmdlet to configure the application log size.The ApplicationLogSize parameter determines the maximum number of records that Access Services should log. A -1 entry means unlimited, and 0 means none. The maximum entry is the maximum integer size (which varies by environment). The default is 3,000 records. A sample modification of the application log size is shown in Listing 23.1.

LISTING 23.1 **Setting the Application Log Size**

```
Set-SPAccessServiceApplication -Identity "Access Ser-
vices"
-ApplicationLogSize 5000
```

Configuring the Cache Timeout

Use the CacheTimeout parameter with the Set-SPAccessServiceApplication cmdlet to configure the cache timeout.The CacheTimeout parameter determines the maximum number of seconds that Access Services should cache data without user activity. A -1 entry means never timeout. The valid range otherwise is 1 to 2073600 (that is, 2,073,600 seconds, equating to 24 days). The default is 300 seconds (5 minutes). A sample modification of the cache timeout is shown in Listing 23.2.

LISTING 23.2 **Setting the Cache Timeout to 10 Minutes**

```
Set-SPAccessServiceApplication -Identity "Access Ser-
vices"
-CacheTimeout 600
```

Modifying the Maximum Columns in a Query

Use the ColumnsMax parameter with the Set-SPAccessServiceApplication cmdlet to configure the maximum number of columns in a query.The ColumnsMax parameter has a default value of 40 and determines the maximum number of columns that can participate in a query and/or be contained in the output of a query. The valid range of values for this parameter is 1 to 255. A sample modification of the maximum amount of columns is shown in Listing 23.3.

LISTING 23.3 **Changing the Maximum Amount of Columns**

```
Set-SPAccessServiceApplication -Identity "Access Ser-
vices"
-ColumnsMax 10
```

Although you may need this to increase the amount of columns allowed, queries typically perform better when there are fewer columns to deal with. If anything, attempt to reduce the amount of columns needed in your Access Services queries.

Modifying the Maximum Calculated Columns in a Query

Use the OutputCalculatedColumnsMax parameter with the Set-SPAccessServiceApplication cmdle to configure the maximum number of calculated columns in a query. The OutputCalculated-ColumnsMax parameter has a default value of 10 and determines the maximum number of calculated columns that can be contained in the output of a query. This value does not include any calculated columns that may be part of SharePoint lists. The valid range of values for this parameter is 0 to 32. A sample modification of the maximum amount of calculated columns is shown in Listing 23.4.

LISTING 23.4 **Changing the Maximum Amount of Columns**

```
Set-SPAccessServiceApplication -Identity "Access Ser-
vices"
-OutputCalculatedColumnsMax 3
```

Calculated columns may improve performance because values are precalculated and then cached. However, having many calculated columns with dynamic data may present performance issues and/or stale data.

Configuring the Maximum Order By Clauses

Use the OrderByMax parameter with the Set-SPAccessServiceApplication cmdlet to configure the maximum number of order by clauses.The OrderByMax parameter has a default value of 4 and determines the maximum number of Order By clauses that can be contained within a query. The valid range of values for this parameter is 0 to 8. A sample modification of the maximum amount of Order By clauses is shown in Listing 23.5.

LISTING 23.5 **Changing the Maximum Amount of Order By Clauses**

```
Set-SPAccessServiceApplication -Identity "Access Ser-
vices"
-OrderByMax 3
```

Order By clauses instantiate sorting algorithms within the query engine. Although this may be optimized with indexes, multiple Order By clauses could place a strain on the query performance. Typically, you only need one Order By to sort the results of your query; however, complex queries may require more than one.

Configuring the Maximum Number of Rows in a Query

Use the RowsMax parameter with the Set-SPAccessServiceApplication cmdlet to configure the maximum number of rows in a query.The RowsMax parameter has a default value of 25000 and determines the maximum number of rows a list that participates in a query may contain and/or the maximum number of rows that may be contained in the results of the query. The valid range of values for this parameter is 1 to 200000. A sample modification of the maximum amount of rows is shown in Listing 23.6.

LISTING 23.6 **Changing the Maximum Number of Rows**

```
Set-SPAccessServiceApplication -Identity "Access Ser-
vices"
-RowsMax 10000
```

Although lists and libraries have been optimized in SharePoint 2013 to allow an "unlimited" amount of items, if you need to deal with entities that contain thousands of rows, you may want to consider migrating the list to an Access table or the entire set of entities to a full-fledged RDBMS such as SQL Server.

Configuring the Maximum Number of Records in an Access Table

Use the RecordsInTableMax parameter with the Set-SPAccessServiceApplication cmdle to configure the maximum number of rows allowed in an Access table.The RecordsInTableMax parameter has a default value of 500000 and determines the maximum number of records that may be contained within an Access table used within Access Services. An entry of -1 means unlimited, whereas the valid range of values for this parameter is 1 to the maximum integer value allowed. A sample modification of the maximum amount of records is shown in Listing 23.7.

LISTING 23.7 **Changing the Maximum Number of Records in a Table**

```
Set-SPAccessServiceApplication -Identity "Access Ser-
vices"
-RecordsInTableMax 100000
```

Configuring the Maximum Number of Sources in a Query

Use the SourcesMax parameter with the Set-SPAccessServiceApplication cmdlet to configure the maximum number of sources allowed in a query.The SourcesMax parameter has a default value of 12 and determines the maximum number of lists that may be used in a query within Access Services. The valid range of values for this parameter is 1 to 20. A sample modification of the maximum amount of sources is shown in Listing 23.8.

LISTING 23.8 **Changing the Maximum Number of Sources in a Query**

```
Set-SPAccessServiceApplication -Identity "Access Ser-
vices"
-SourcesMax 8
```

Enabling/Disabling the Use of Outer Joins

Use the OuterJoinsAllowed switch parameter with the Set-SPAccessServiceApplication cmdlet to enable or disable the use of outer joins.By default, the Access Services service application is configured to allow outer joins within queries. Because OuterJoinsAllowed is a switch parameter, you may use it with a $false setting to disable outer joins, as shown in Listing 23.9.

LISTING 23.9 **Disabling Outer Joins in Queries**

```
Set-SPAccessServiceApplication -Identity "Access Ser-
vices"
-OuterJoinsAllowed:$false
```

You may use –OuterJoinsAllowed by itself to enable this setting or with a $true value, as shown in Listing 23.10.

LISTING 23.10 **Enabling Outer Joins in Queries**

```
Set-SPAccessServiceApplication -Identity "Access Ser-
vices"
-OuterJoinsAllowed:$true
```

Allowing/Restricting Non-Remotable Queries

Use the NonRemotableQueriesAllowed switch parameter with the Set-SPAccessServiceApplication cmdlet to allow or restrict non-remotable queries.Non-remotable queries are queries that cannot be remotely executed within the database. By default, the Access Services service application is configured to allow non-remotable queries. Because NonRemotableQueriesAllowed is a switch parameter, you may use it with a $false setting to disable non-remotable queries, as shown in Listing 23.11.

LISTING 23.11 **Disabling Non-Remotable Queries**

```
Set-SPAccessServiceApplication -Identity "Access Ser-
vices"
-NonRemotableQueriesAllowed:$false
```

You may use –NonRemotableQueriesAllowed by itself to enable this setting or with a $true value, as shown in Listing 23.12.

```
Set-SPAccessServiceApplication -Identity "Access Ser-
vices"
-NonRemotableQueriesAllowed:$true
```

Configuring Memory Utilization

Use the PrivateBytesMax parameter with the Set-SPAccessServiceApplication cmdlet to configure memory utilization.By default, Access Services is configured to use up to 50% of the physical memory of the application server that is hosting the service application. This is denoted by a -1 value for the Maximum Private Bytes setting. To change this value, you may use the PrivateBytesMax parameter with a value between 1 and the maximum amount of physical memory available. A sample modification of memory usage using the Set-SPAccessServiceApplication cmdlet is shown in Listing 23.13.

LISTING 23.13 **Modifying the Memory Usage of Access Services**

```
Set-SPAccessServiceApplication -Identity "Access Ser-
vices"
-PrivateBytesMax 1024
```

Configuring Session Memory Utilization

Use the SessionMemoryMax parameter with the Set-SPAccessServiceApplication cmdlet to configure session memory limits.By default, Access Services is configured to use up 64MB of memory per session. To change this value, you may use the SessionMemoryMax parameter with a value between 1 and 4095. A sample modification of session memory usage using the Set-SPAccessServiceApplication cmdlet is shown in Listing 23.14.

LISTING 23.14 **Modifying the Session Memory Usage of Access Services**

```
Set-SPAccessServiceApplication -Identity "Access Ser-
vices"
-SessionMemoryMax 50
```

This is the maximum amount of memory that a session will use. Normally only a small amount is needed, so the default limit of 64MB should be plenty. If sessions are using more memory than expected, you may want to investigate what operations are being performed during typical sessions.

Configuring User Sessions

Use the SessionsPerUserMax or SessionsPerAnonymousUserMax parameter with the Set-SPAccessServiceApplication cmdlet to configure user sessions.The SessionsPerUserMax and SessionsPerAnonymousUserMax settings determine the maximum amount of sessions that can be created per user. Once the limit is reached, older sessions are deleted to make room for new ones. The default per user is 10, whereas the default per anonymous user is 25. An entry of -1 denotes unlimited, and the valid range otherwise is 1 to the maximum integer value allowed. An example of setting both user session values is shown in Listing 23.15.

LISTING 23.15 **Modifying the Amount of Sessions Per User**

```
Set-SPAccessServiceApplication -Identity "Access Ser-
vices"
-SessionsPerUserMax 5 -SessionsPerAnonymousUserMax 5
```

Limiting Template Sizes

Use the TemplateSizeMax parameter with the Set-SPAccessServiceApplication cmdlet to configure the maximum template size.The TemplateSizeMax parameter may be used to configure the maximum size of an Access template. The default is 30MB. An entry of -1 denotes no limit, and a valid entry is any positive integer. An example for modifying the template size limit is shown in Listing 23.16.

LISTING 23.16 **Modifying the Template Size Limit**

```
Set-SPAccessServiceApplication -Identity "Access Ser-
vices"
-TemplateSizeMax 15
```

Modifying Access Services Databases

This chapter covers the basic or more common cmdlets for creating and using Access Services objects. For more advance scripting and modifications of these objects, the following cmdlets are available:

- Get-SPAccessServicesDatabase
- Get-SPAccessServicesDatabaseServer
- Set-SPAccessServicesDatabaseServer
- Get-SPAccessServicesDatabaseServerGroup
- Get-SPAccessServicesDatabaseServerGroupMapping
- Set-SPAccessServicesDatabaseServerGroupMapping
- New-SPAccessServicesDatabaseServer
- Remove-SPAccessServicesDatabaseServer
- Reset-SPAccessServicesDatabasePassword

Intentionally BLANK

CHAPTER 24

Visio Graphics Services

Configuring the Unattended Service Account

Visio Graphics Services uses the Secure Store Service to facilitate the use of an unattended service account. You must first create a Secure Store Service entry with an Application ID for Visio Graphics Services.

Once an Application ID has been established, you may use the Set-SPVisioExternalData cmdlet to configure the unattended service account for Visio Graphic Services as shown in Listing 24.1.

LISTING 24.1 **Configure the Unattended Service Account**

```
Set-SPVisioExternalData -VisioServiceApplication "Vi-
sio Graphics Service" -
UnattendedServiceAccountApplicationID "Secure Store
Visio Graphics"
```

Creating a New Safe Data Provider

The New-SPVisioSafeDataProvider may be used to create a new safe data provider that Excel workbooks can access via a data connection. Provide the provider information and the Visio Graphics Service instance as shown in Listing 24.2.

LISTING 24.2 **Create a New Safe Data Provider**

```
New-SPVisioSafeDataProvider
-VisioServiceApplication "Visio Graphics Service"
-DataProviderID "Custom Visio DB"
-DataProviderType 2
```

The –DataProviderID is an identifier for the data provider. The –DataProviderType can be any of the following integer values:

- 1 - OLE DB
- 2 – SQL Server
- 3 – ODBC
- 4 – ODBC with DSN
- 5 – SharePoint List
- 6 – Custom

Upon successful creation of the new safe data provider, a summary of the properties are displayed as shown in Figure 24.1.

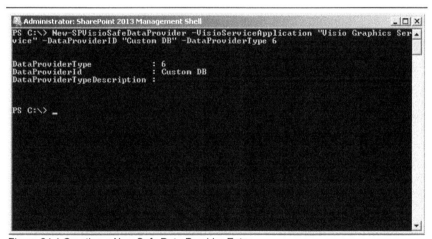

Figure 24.1 Creating a New Safe Data Provider Entry

The DataProviderTypeDescription is blank since the New-SPVisioSafeDataProvider cmdlet does not have a parameter to include a description. To update the description you need to use the Set-SPVisioSafeDataProvider cmdlet.

Displaying All Safe Data Providers

Using the Get-SPVisioSafeDataProvider with the VisioServiceApplication parameter as shown in Listing 24.3 displays all configured safe data providers.

LISTING 24.3 **Displaying All Safe Data Providers**

```
Get-SPVisioSafeDataProvider -VisioServiceApplication
"Visio Graphics Service"
```

Retrieving a Specific Safe Data Provider

The Get-SPVisioSafeDataProvider cmdlet can be used to retrieve a specific safe data provider using the VisioServiceApplication and data provider parameters as shown in listing 24.4

LISTING 24.4 **Assigning a Variable to a Specific Data Provider**

```
$dataProvider =
Get-SPVisioSafeDataProvider -VisioServiceApplication
"Visio Graphics Service" -DataProviderID "Custom DB"
-DataProviderType 6
```

This cmdlet uses both the DataProviderID and the DataProviderType to identify the safe data provider. If one or the other is excluded, no results will be returned.

Removing a Safe Data Provider

The Remove-SPVisioSafeDataProvider cmdlet allows you to remove a specific safe data provider from Visio Graphics Services. This cmdlet uses both the DataProviderID and the DataProviderType to identify the safe data provider as shown in Listing 24.5.

LISTING 24.5 **Example Script for Removing a Safe Data Provider**

```
Remove-SPVisioSafeDataProvider -
VisioServiceApplication "Visio Graphics Service" -
DataProviderID "Custom DB" -DataProviderType 6
```

Modifying the Description of a Data Provider

You may use the Set-SPVisioSafeDataProvider cmdlet to modify the description of a data provider. This cmdlet uses both the DataProviderID and the DataProviderType to identify the safe data provider as shown in Listing 24.6.

LISTING 24.5 **Modifying the Description of a Safe Data Provider**

```
Set-SPVisioSafeDataProvider

-VisioServiceApplication "Visio Graphics Service"

-DataProviderID "Custom Visio DB"

-DataProviderType 4

-Description "Custom DB Provider"
```

Configuring Visio Performance Settings

Use the Set-SPVisioPerformance cmdlet to configure the performance settings of Visio Graphics Services. All parameters for this cmdlet are required. Therefore, you need to provide a value for each setting as shown in Listing 24.6.

LISTING 24.6 **Configuring the Visio Performance Settings**

```
Set-SPVisioPerformance -VisioServiceApplication "Vi-
sio Graphics Service" -MaxDiagramCacheAge 30 -MaxDiagramSize 5 -
MaxRecalcDuration 60 -MinDiagramCacheAge 10
```

The –MaxDiagramCacheAge determines the maximum amount of minutes a diagram should be cached. A longer cache age reduces memory and CPU utilization since the diagrams are not refreshed as often. The default value is 60 minutes, however the valid range of values for this parameter are between 0 and 34560 minutes (equating to 24 days).

The –MaxDiagramSize determines the largest amount of megabytes a Visio diagram can be to be processed by the Visio Graphics Service. The default value is 5 megabytes, however the valid range of values for this parameter are between 1 and 50 megabytes.

The –MaxRecalcDuration determines the maximum amount of seconds that the Visio Graphics Service should spend recalculating a diagram. The default is 60 seconds while the parameter range can be from 1 to 120 seconds. Any recalculations taking longer than this setting will timeout.

The –MinDiagramCacheAge determines the minimum amount of minutes a diagram should be cached. A longer cache age reduces memory and CPU utilization since the diagrams are not refreshed as often. The default value is 5 minutes, however the valid range of values for this parameter are between 0 and 34560 minutes (equating to 24 days).

CHAPTER 25

Word Automation Services

Configuring the Conversion Processes

Use the ActiveProcesses parameter with the Set-SPWordConversionServiceApplication cmdlet to configure the conversion processes. The ActiveProcesses parameter determines the how many active conversion processes can occur on each server running the Word Services service application. The default is only one process. The valid entries range from 1 to 1000. A sample modification of the active conversion processes is shown in Listing 25.1.

LISTING 25.1 **Setting the Active Conversion Processes**

```
Set-SPWordConversionServiceApplication

-Identity "Word Automation Services" -ActiveProcesses
10
```

Configuring Conversion Throughput

Use the TimerJobFrequency and ConversionsPerInstance parameters with the Set-SPWordConversionServiceApplication cmdlet to configure conversion throughput. The conversion throughput parameters TimerJobFrequency and ConversionsPerInstance correspond to the Word Services configuration settings, as shown in Figure 25.1.

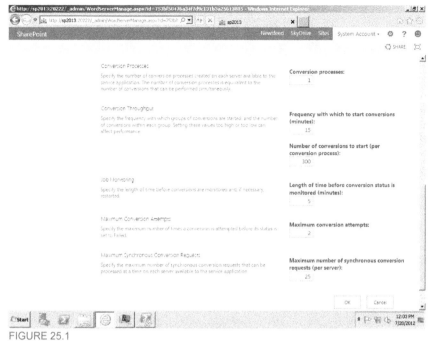

FIGURE 25.1

Conversion throughput configuration settings in Central Administration

To get to these properties, from Central Admin, click on the Manage Service Applications link under Application Management. Locate the Word Services entry and highlight the connection (the indented instance) and then click on the Properties button from the top ribbon bar.

The TimerJobFrequency parameter determines how often the conversion process should be started using the corresponding service timer job. The default is 15 minutes, and the valid range maybe any number of minutes between 1 and 59.

The ConversionsPerInstance parameter determines how many conversions may be processed per instance. The number of instances can be configured using the ActiveProcesses parameter, as explained in the previous section. The default value is 300 conversions.

A sample command line for setting the conversion throughput values is shown in Listing 25.2.

LISTING 25.2 **Configuring the Conversion Throughput Values**

```
Set-SPWordConversionServiceApplication

    -Identity "Word Automation Services"

    -TimerJobFrequency 5

    -ConversionsPerInstance 100
```

Configuring Supported Document Formats

Use the AddSupportedFormats and RemoveSupportedFormats parameters with the Set-SPWordConversionServiceApplication cmdlet to configure supported document types.By default, all available document file formats are supported within Word Services. You may use the AddSupportedFormats or RemoveSupportedFormats parameter with the Set-SPWordConversionServiceApplication cmdlet to modify which set of formats is supported.

Both parameters take a comma-separated list of valid document formats. The recognized values are as follows:

- **docx**—Open XML Document. This essentially is any Word 2010 or Word 2007 document and includes .docx, .docm, .dotx, and .dotm documents.
- **doc**—Word 97-2003 Documents. Provides support for older Word documents with .doc or .dot extensions.
- **rtf**—Rich text Format. Only supports .rtf files.
- **mht**—Web Page. Any HTML-based web page, including .htm, .html, .mht, and .mhtml documents.

> **xml**—Word 2003 XML Document. Any Word 2003 document saved as an .xml file.

As an example of how these parameters operate, removing "doc" also removes support for .dot documents. The supported formats are grouped together and cannot be broken apart. These groups correspond to the available options available through Central Administration, as shown in Figure 25.2. Sample command lines are shown in Listing 25.3.

LISTING 25.3 **Modifying the Supported File Formats**

```
Set-SPWordConversionServiceApplication
       -Identity "Word Automation Services"
       -RemoveSupportedFormats rtf,mht

Set-SPWordConversionServiceApplication
       -Identity "Word Automation Services"
       -AddSupportedFormats docx,doc
```

FIGURE 25.2
Supported document options for Word Services

253

You may use quotes around a single file format; however, when you are providing a comma-separated list of formats, quotes cannot be used. No errors will be presented, although the operation will not modify the settings.

Modifying Database Information

Use the database parameters with the Set-SPWordConversionServiceApplication cmdlet to modify the Word Services database information. Three database parameters may be used to configure the database settings for Word Services: DatabaseServer, DatabaseName, and DatabaseCredential.

The DatabaseCredential parameter is only used if the authorization is performed through SQL Authentication. Even though all of these parameters are optional overall, if the DatabaseCredential parameter is used, then the DatabaseServer and DatabaseName become required. A sample modification of the database settings is shown in Listing 25.4.

LISTING 25.4 **Changing the Database Configuration for Word Services**

```
Set-SPWordConversionServiceApplication

        -Identity "Word Automation Services"

        -DatabaseServer SP2013

        -DatabaseName WordServicesDB

        -DatabaseCredential (Get-Credential)
```

If the database that is described within the DatabaseName parameter does not exist, it will be created automatically.

Configuring Job Monitoring

Use the ConversionTimeout parameter with the Set-SPWordConversionServiceApplication cmdlet to configure job monitoring. This value is the number of minutes a conversion should be in progress before the timer job restarts the conversion. The default is 5 minutes. The valid range of values is 1 to 60 minutes. A sample modification of the job monitoring setting is shown in Listing 25.5.

LISTING 25.5 **Configuring the Job Monitoring Timeout Setting**

```
Set-SPWordConversionServiceApplication

    -Identity "Word Automation Services"

    -ConversionTimeout 15
```

This is different from the actual configurations that determine how long a conversion can be nonresponsive or how long a conversion should run. Those values can be modified using the parameters explained in the next section.

Configuring Conversion Timeouts

Use the KeepAliveTimeout or MaximumConversionTime parameters with the Set-SPWordConversionServiceApplication cmdlet to configure conversion timeouts.

Provide the KeepAliveTimeout parameter to determine how many seconds a process can be nonresponsive before it is terminated. The valid values for this setting are from 10 to 60 seconds and the default is 30 seconds.

Provide the MaximumConversionTime parameter to determine how long a conversion should continue running. The default is 300 seconds, whereas the range starts at 60 seconds and can go up to the maximum allowed integer value. A sample modification of the conversion timeout setting is shown in Listing 25.6.

LISTING 25.6 **Changing the Conversion Timeout Settings**

```
Set-SPWordConversionServiceApplication -Identity
"Word Automation Services" -KeepAliveTimeout 45 -
MaximumConversionTime 120
```

Configuring Maximum Conversion Attempts

Use the MaximumConversionAttempts parameter with the Set-SPWordConversionServiceApplication cmdlet to configure the maximum number of conversion attempts in Word Services. The value provided determines how many attempts should be taken before a conversion is considered a failure. The default is 2 (attempts) and the range of valid values is 1 to 10. A sample modification of the maximum conversion attempts setting is shown in Listing 25.7.

LISTING 25.7 **Changing the Maximum Conversion Attempts Setting**

```
Set-SPWordConversionServiceApplication -Identity
"Word Automation Services" -MaximumConversionAttempts
5
```

Configuring Maximum Memory Usage

Use the MaximumMemoryUsage parameter with the Set-SPWordConversionServiceApplication cmdlet to configure the maximum memory usage of Word Services. The value provided determines how much memory Word Services can use on the server. The default is 100 (percent), whereas the range of valid values is 10 to 100. A sample modification of the maximum memory usage setting is shown in Listing 25.8.

LISTING 25.8 **Changing the Maximum Memory Usage to 60%**

```
Set-SPWordConversionServiceApplication

-Identity "Word Automation Services"

-MaximumMemoryUsage 60
```

Disabling Word 97–2003 Document Scanning

Use the DisableBinaryFileScan parameter with the Set-SPWordConversionServiceApplication cmdlet to disable older Word version document scanning..DisableBinaryFileScan is a switch parameter. By default it is false, and Word Services performs additional checks on older Word documents (Word 97–2003). If you trust all sources of Word documents, you may disable this additional scanning by using Set-SPWordConversionServiceApplication with the DisableBinaryFileScan switch parameter, as shown in Listing 25.9.

LISTING 25.9 **Disabling the Scanning of Word 97–2003 Documents**

```
Set-SPWordConversionServiceApplication

    -Identity "Word Automation Services"

    -DisableBinaryFileScan
```

As long as all sources are trusted, it is a good idea to disable scanning to improve performance of Word Services against those documents. To enable scanning, use the same parameter with a $false value, as shown in Listing 25.10.

LISTING 25.10 **Enabling the Scanning of Word 97–2003 Documents**

```
Set-SPWordConversionServiceApplication

-Identity "Word Automation Services" -
DisableBinaryFileScan:$false
```

Disabling Embedded Fonts in Conversions

Use the DisableEmbeddedFonts parameter with the Set-SPWordConversionServiceApplication cmdlet to disable embedded fonts in Word Services conversions.DisableEmbeddedFonts is a switch parameter. By default it is false, and Word Services supports the conversion of embedded fonts within Word documents. You may disable this support by using Set-SPWordConversionServiceApplication with the DisableEmbeddedFonts switch parameter, as shown in Listing 25.11.

LISTING 25.11 **Disabling Embedded Font Support**

```
Set-SPWordConversionServiceApplication

-Identity "Word Automation Services" -
DisableEmbeddedFonts
```

Unless you are experiencing issues with embedded fonts, you should be able to keep this setting enabled. To enable embedded font support, use the same parameter with a $false value, as shown in Listing 25.12.

LISTING 25.12 **Enabling Embedded Font Support**

```
Set-SPWordConversionServiceApplication

-Identity "Word Automation Services" -
DisableEmbeddedFonts:$false
```

Configuring the Recycle Process Threshold

Use the RecycleProcessThreshold parameter with the Set-SPWordConversionServiceApplication cmdlet to configure the recycle process threshold.The RecycleProcessThreshold parameter allows you to specify the number of documents each conversion process can convert before the process is recycled. The default value is 100 (documents), whereas the valid range of values is 1 to 1000. A sample threshold modification is shown in Listing 25.13.

LISTING 25.13 **Changing the Recycle Threshold**

```
Set-SPWordConversionServiceApplication

        -Identity "Word Automation Services"

        -RecycleProcessThreshold 300
```

Intentionally BLANK

CHAPTER 26

Office Web Apps

This chapter explores new cmdlets in SharePoint 2013 that may be used to configure Web Application Open Platform Interface Protocol (WOPI) applications in SharePoint. The SharePoint 2013 WOPI cmdlets allow you to create new bindings and configure WOPI settings.

From the WOPI specification by Microsoft, *"WOPI defines a set of operations that enables a client to access and change files stored by a server. This allows the client to render files and provide file editing functionality for files stored by the server."*

The full specification and details may be found here:
http://msdn.microsoft.com/en-us/library/hh622722(v=office.12).aspx

Essentially the WOPI provides a method of rendering specific types of files in a browser without the need for a client application. In other words, you may render Word documents within Internet Explorer without having Microsoft Word installed on your machine.

While the WOPI settings are generic and used for any WOPI-type application, server, and/or services, the Microsoft Office WOPI applications are named Office Web Apps. In order to use Office Web Apps locally with SharePoint 2013, you must have a dedicated server running Office Web Apps Server.

Creating a New WOPI Binding in SharePoint

The New-SPWOPIBinding cmdlet creates a new binding to associate file types or applications with SharePoint. Essentially if you have an Office Web App server running, all you need to do is execute this cmdlet with the server name as shown in Listing 25.1.

LISTING 25.1 **Creating the WOPI Binding in SharePoint**

```
New-SPWOPIBinding -ServerName "Office.mycompany.com"
```

This automatically associates the supported file extensions and applications within SharePoint. The current supported applications are Word, Excel, PowerPoint, and OneNote.

You may also use the -Application parameter to bind a specific application as shown in Listing 25.2. The valid parameter values are:

- **Excel**
- **OneNote**
- **PowerPoint**
- **Word**

LISTING 25.2 **Creating the WOPI Binding for a Specific Application**

```
New-SPWOPIBinding -ServerName "Office.mycompany.com"
- Application "Word"
```

Reviewing Current SharePoint WOPI Bindings

You may use the Get-SPWOPIBinding cmdlet to retrieve a list of bindings that were created as a result from the New-SPWOPIBinding cmdlet explained in the previous section. You may use the cmdlet without any parameters or you may provide one or more of the following parameters to narrow the list:

- **Action** - string that specifies a specific action to return (e.g. "view', "edit")
- **Application** - string that specifies a specific application to return (e.g. "Excel")
- **Extension** - string that specifies a specific file extension to return (e.g. "doc, xls")
- **Server** - string that specifies a specific WOPI server to return
- **WOPIZone** - string that specifies a specific zone to return

Configuring the Default Action for an Application

The Set-SPWOPIBinding cmdlet is used to set the default action of applications. This is achieved by providing the -DefaultAction switch parameter along with a WOPIBinding object via the -Identity parameter.

Use the Get-SPWOPIBinding cmdlet, explained in the previous section, to set a variable to a specific binding or pipe the results into the Set-SPWOPIBinding cmdlet as show in in Listing 25.3

LISTING 25.3 **Configuring the Default Action for Excel Documents in SharePoint**

```
Get-SPWOPIBinding -Action "View" -Application "Excel"
| Set-SPWOPIBinding -DefaultAction:$true
```

Removing WOPI Bindings from SharePoint

The Remove-SPWOPIBinding cmdlet has three different parameter sets that may be used to remove bindings. The simplest set is used to remove all bindings and only needs to the -All switch parameter as shown in Listing 25.4.

LISTING 25.4 **Removing All WOPI Bindings from SharePoint**

```
Remove-SPWOPIBinding -All
```

Provide a specific binding using the identity pipe parameter to re-move a specific binding as shown in Listing 25.5 or simply provide the same parameters to Remove-SPWOPIBinding as you would to get the binding as shown in Listing 25.6.

LISTING 25.5 **Removing a Specific Binding Using the Identity Pipe**

```
Get-SPWOPIBinding -Application "Excel" | Remove-
SPWOPIBinding
```

LISTING 25.6 **Removing a Specific Binding Using Parameters**

```
Remove-SPWOPIBinding -Application "Excel"
```

You may use the following parameters to identify a specific bind-ing:

  ▷ **Action** - string that specifies a specific action to return (e.g. "view', "edit")

- **Application** - string that specifies a specific application to return (e.g. "Excel")
- **Extension** - string that specifies a specific file extension to return (e.g. "doc, xls")
- **Server** - string that specifies a specific WOPI server to return
- **WOPIZone** - string that specifies a specific zone to return

Configuring the WOPI SharePoint Zone

The Set-SPWOPIZone cmdlet is used solely to configure the zone in which SharePoint uses to navigate the browser to the WOPI application. The zone is specified using the -Zone parameter and may be one of the following values:

- **Internal-HTTP**
- **Internal-HTTPS**
- **External-HTTP**
- **External-HTTPS**

Disabling Certain WOPI Actions

The New-SPWOPISuppressionSetting cmdlet is used to disable Office Web App functionality for the specified action, file extension, and/or programmatic identifier. You may view the current bindings using the Get-SPWOPIBinding cmdlet and retrieve the available values for the parameters. Typically, the -Action and -Extension parameters are used together to suppress an action for a particular document type as shown in Listing 25.7

LISTING 25.7 **Suppressing an Action on a Specific File Extension**

```
New-SPWOPISuppressionSetting  -Action "View" -
Extension "xls"
```

To view current suppression settings, use the Get-SPWOPISuppressionSetting cmdlet without any parameters. You may also remove any suppression setting by using the Remove-SPWOPISuppressionSetting cmdlet with the action and extension or by providing the identity of the specific suppression setting.

Resolving Invalid Proof Signatures

WOPI uses a public key to for communication between the SharePoint farm and the Office Web Apps server. Sometimes keys become unsynchronized and need to be reset. Use the Update-SPWOPIProofKey cmdlet with the optional -ServerName parameter to update the public key and resolve any invalid proof signature issues. An example is shown in Listing 25.8

LISTING 25.8 **Updating the WOPI Public Key**

```
Update-SPWOPIProofKey
        -ServerName "Office.mycompany.com"
```

APPENDIXES

Appendix A - Upgrade and Migration
Appendix B - Enterprise Search Reference
Appendix C - App Management Service Reference

Upgrade and Migration

This appendix presents several SharePoint cmdlets that may be used during the upgrade and migration process when migrating from MOSS 2007 or SharePoint 2010 to SharePoint 2013.

Test-SPContentDatabase

When performing a SharePoint migration, part of the operation is to back up the MOSS 2007 or SharePoint 2010 content database(s) and then restore them on your SharePoint 2013 SQL Server. You then should test the content database(s) against your new Share-Point 2013 web application to determine if there are any issues.

The syntax for the above scenario is as follows:

```
Test-SPContentDatabase
    -Name <name of content database>
    -WebApplication <name of web application to
    test against>
```

By default, the current SQL Server instance will be used but you may specify an instance by using the –ServerInstance parameter and passing in the SQL Server instance.

Upgrade-SPContentDatabase

Once the content database has been tested and all issues have been resolved, it then can be attached to the SharePoint farm using the Mount-SPContentDatabase cmdlet. The upgrade command will not execute until the content database is actually attached. Once attached, you may execute the upgrade command using the following syntax:

```
Upgrade-SPContentDatabase -Name <name of content da-
tabase>
```

```
-WebApplication <name of web application hosting con-
tent database>
```

Again, by default, the current SQL Server instance will be used but
you may specify an instance by using the –ServerInstance parameter and passing in the SQL Server instance.

Upgrade-SPFarm

To initiate the upgrade process on the local farm, use the Upgrade-
SPFarm cmdlet. There are no required parameters so you may run
this as is.

```
Upgrade-SPFarm
```

Test-SPSite

It is essential to insure that all site collections are considered
healthy. Therefore you may run health analyzer tests against a site
collection by using Test-SPSite and providing the URL of the site
collection as the Identity.

```
Test-SPSite -Identity <URL or GUID of Site Collec-
tion> [-RuleId <rule GUID>] [-RunAlways <optional
switch parameter>]
```

Repair-SPSite

After testing a site collection, if repairs need to be made, you may
use the Repair-SPSite cmdlet which has similar parameters as the
Test-SPSite cmdlet.

```
Repair-SPSite -Identity <URL or GUID of Site Collec-
tion> [-RuleId <rule GUID>] [-RunAlways <optional
switch parameter>]
```

Upgrade-SPSite

To start the upgrade process on a particular site collection, use the
Upgrade-SPSite cmdlet and provide the GUID or URL for the -
Identity parameter.

```
Upgrade-SPSite -Identity <URL or GUID of Site Collec-
tion>
[-Unthrottled] [-VersionUpgrade]
```

The -Unthrottled switch parameter acts a "force" command and
performs the upgrade on the specified site collection regardless of
how many site collections are being upgraded. The -
VersionUpgrade switch parameter performs and upgrade of the site
collection to the next build level (e.g. 12 to 14, 14 to 15).

Additional Upgrade Cmdlets

In addition to the common upgrade cmdlets for SharePoint migration, the following cmdlets are available for more granular upgrading:

- Get-SPPendingUpgradeActions
- Get-SPSiteUpgradeSessionInfo
- Get-SPUpgradeActions

- Remove-SPSiteUpgradeSessionInfo
- Request-SPUpgradeEvaluationSite
- Copy-SPSite

Enterprise Search Reference

This appendix presents all of the Enterprise Search related cmdlets that are available. Enterprise Search consists of many areas including crawling, querying, metadata, etc. and therefore has a plethora of cmdlets.

Administrative

There are only two cmdlets that fall into this classification:

- Get-SPEnterpriseSearchStatus
- New-SPEnterpriseSearchAdminComponent

Crawling

The crawling cmdlets may be used to tweak the crawl settings and configurations. The Get-based cmdlets are listed here:

- Get-SPEnterpriseSearchCrawlContentSource
- Get-SPEnterpriseSearchCrawlCustomConnector
- Get-SPEnterpriseSearchCrawlDatabase
- Get-SPEnterpriseSearchCrawlExtension
- Get-SPEnterpriseSearchCrawlMapping
- Get-SPEnterpriseSearchCrawlRule

Create new crawl objects (e.g. components, content sources, databases) using these cmdlets:

- New-SPEnterpriseSearchCrawlComponent
- New-SPEnterpriseSearchCrawlContentSource
- New-SPEnterpriseSearchCrawlCustomConnector
- New-SPEnterpriseSearchCrawlDatabase
- New-SPEnterpriseSearchCrawlExtension

- New-SPEnterpriseSearchCrawlMapping
- New-SPEnterpriseSearchCrawlRule

You may remove crawl objects, permissions, and rules using these cmdlets:

- Remove-SPEnterpriseSearchCrawlContentSource
- Remove-SPEnterpriseSearchCrawlCustomConnector
- Remove-SPEnterpriseSearchCrawlDatabase
- Remove-SPEnterpriseSearchCrawlExtension
- Remove-SPEnterpriseSearchCrawlMapping
- Remove-SPEnterpriseSearchCrawlRule
- Remove-SPEnterpriseSearchCrawlLogReadPermission
- Remove-SPEnterpriseSearchCrawlLogReadPermission

There are only a handful of cmdlets that may be used to config crawl settings:

- Set-SPEnterpriseSearchCrawlContentSource
- Set-SPEnterpriseSearchCrawlDatabase
- Set-SPEnterpriseSearchCrawlRule
- Set-SPEnterpriseSearchCrawlLogReadPermission

Metadata

The full list of search metadata cmdlets are listed here.

- Get-SPEnterpriseSearchMetadataCategory
- Get-SPEnterpriseSearchMetadataCrawledProperty
- Get-SPEnterpriseSearchMetadataManagedProperty
- Get-SPEnterpriseSearchMetadataMapping
- Get-SPEnterpriseSearchPropertyRuleCollection
- Get-SPEnterpriseSearchPropertyRule
- New-SPEnterpriseSearchMetadataCategory
- New-SPEnterpriseSearchMetadataCrawledProperty
- New-SPEnterpriseSearchMetadataManagedProperty
- New-SPEnterpriseSearchMetadataMapping
- Remove-SPEnterpriseSearchMetadataCategory
- Remove-SPEnterpriseSearchMetadataManagedProperty
- Remove-SPEnterpriseSearchMetadataMapping
- Set-SPEnterpriseSearchMetadataCategory
- Set-SPEnterpriseSearchMetadataCrawledProperty
- Set-SPEnterpriseSearchMetadataManagedProperty
- Set-SPEnterpriseSearchMetadataMapping

Miscellaneous

There are several cmdlets that may be used to tweak certain areas and settings of Enterprise Search but can't be classified into a specific area. These cmdlets are as follows:

- Get-SPEnterpriseSearchLanguageResourcePhrase
- Get-SPEnterpriseSearchSiteHitRule
- Get-SPEnterpriseSearchLinksDatabase
- Get-SPEnterpriseSearchFileFormat
- Get-SPEnterpriseSearchComponent
- Get-SPEnterpriseSearchServiceApplicationBackupStore
- Get-SPEnterpriseSearchVssDataPath
- Get-SPEnterpriseSearchContentEnrichmentConfiguration
- Get-SPEnterpriseSearchLinguisticComponentsStatus
- Get-SPEnterpriseSearchHostController
- Import-SPEnterpriseSearchCustomExtractionDictionary
- New-SPEnterpriseSearchLanguageResourcePhrase
- New-SPEnterpriseSearchSiteHitRule
- New-SPEnterpriseSearchLinksDatabase
- New-SPEnterpriseSearchFileFormat
- New-SPEnterpriseSearchAnalyticsProcessingComponent
- New-SPEnterpriseSearchContentEnrichmentConfiguration
- Remove-SPEnterpriseSearchContentEnrichmentConfiguration
- Remove-SPEnterpriseSearchLanguageResourcePhrase
- Remove-SPEnterpriseSearchSiteHitRule
- Remove-SPEnterpriseSearchTenantSchema
- Remove-SPEnterpriseSearchTenantConfiguration
- Remove-SPEnterpriseSearchLinksDatabase

- ▸ Remove-SPEnterpriseSearchFileFormat
- ▸ Repartition-SPEnterpriseSearchLinksDatabases
- ▸ Set-SPEnterpriseSearchPrimaryHostController
- ▸ Set-SPEnterpriseSearchLinguisticComponentsStatus
- ▸ Set-SPEnterpriseSearchContentEnrichmentConfiguration
- ▸ Set-SPEnterpriseSearchLinksDatabase

Querying

To manage, tweak, and configure the querying in your SharePoint farm, the following cmdlets are available:

- ▸ Get-SPEnterpriseSearchQueryAndSiteSettingsService
- ▸ Get-SPEnterpriseSearchQueryAndSiteSettingsServiceInstance
- ▸ Get-SPEnterpriseSearchQueryAndSiteSettingsServiceProxy
- ▸ Get-SPEnterpriseSearchQueryAuthority
- ▸ Get-SPEnterpriseSearchQueryDemoted
- ▸ Get-SPEnterpriseSearchQueryKeyword
- ▸ Get-SPEnterpriseSearchQueryScope
- ▸ Get-SPEnterpriseSearchQueryScopeRule
- ▸ Get-SPEnterpriseSearchQuerySuggestionCandidates
- ▸ Get-SPEnterpriseSearchRankingModel
- ▸ Get-SPEnterpriseSearchSecurityTrimmer
- ▸ Get-SPEnterpriseSearchResultItemType
- ▸ Get-SPEnterpriseSearchQuerySpellingCorrection
- ▸ Import-SPEnterpriseSearchPopularQueries
- ▸ Import-SPEnterpriseSearchThesaurus
- ▸ New-SPEnterpriseSearchQueryAuthority

- New-SPEnterpriseSearchQueryDemoted
- New-SPEnterpriseSearchQueryKeyword
- New-SPEnterpriseSearchQueryScope
- New-SPEnterpriseSearchQueryScopeRule
- New-SPEnterpriseSearchRankingModel
- New-SPEnterpriseSearchSecurityTrimmer
- New-SPEnterpriseSearchResultItemType
- Remove-SPEnterpriseSearchQueryAuthority
- Remove-SPEnterpriseSearchQueryDemoted
- Remove-SPEnterpriseSearchQueryKeyword
- Remove-SPEnterpriseSearchQueryScope
- Remove-SPEnterpriseSearchQueryScopeRule
- Remove-SPEnterpriseSearchRankingModel
- Remove-SPEnterpriseSearchSecurityTrimmer
- Remove-SPEnterpriseSearchResultItemType
- Set-SPEnterpriseSearchQueryAuthority
- Set-SPEnterpriseSearchQueryKeyword
- Set-SPEnterpriseSearchQueryScope
- Set-SPEnterpriseSearchQueryScopeRule
- Set-SPEnterpriseSearchRankingModel
- Set-SPEnterpriseSearchResultItemType
- Set-SPEnterpriseSearchQuerySpellingCorrection
- Start-SPEnterpriseSearchQueryAndSiteSettingsServiceInstance
- Stop-SPEnterpriseSearchQueryAndSiteSettingsServiceInstance

Service Application

The search service application also comes loaded with configuration cmdlets listed here.

- Backup-SPEnterpriseSearchServiceApplicationIndex
- Get-SPEnterpriseSearchOwner
- Get-SPEnterpriseSearchService
- Get-SPEnterpriseSearchServiceApplication
- Get-SPEnterpriseSearchServiceApplicationProxy
- Get-SPEnterpriseSearchServiceInstance
- New-SPEnterpriseSearchServiceApplication
- New-SPEnterpriseSearchServiceApplicationProxy
- Remove-SPEnterpriseSearchServiceApplication
- Remove-SPEnterpriseSearchServiceApplicationProxy
- Restore-SPEnterpriseSearchServiceApplication
- Resume-SPEnterpriseSearchServiceApplication
- Restore-SPEnterpriseSearchServiceApplicationIndex
- Remove-SPEnterpriseSearchServiceApplicationSiteSettings
- Set-SPEnterpriseSearchService
- Set-SPEnterpriseSearchServiceApplication
- Set-SPEnterpriseSearchServiceApplicationProxy
- Start-SPEnterpriseSearchServiceInstance
- Stop-SPEnterpriseSearchServiceInstance
- Suspend-SPEnterpriseSearchServiceApplication
- Suspend-SPEnterpriseSearchServiceApplication
- Upgrade-SPEnterpriseSearchServiceApplication
- Upgrade-SPEnterpriseSearchServiceApplicationSiteSettings

Topology

In SharePoint 2013, you may now generate and configure the search topology on your farm using these cmdlets:

- Export-SPEnterpriseSearchTopology
- Get-SPEnterpriseSearchTopology
- Import-SPEnterpriseSearchTopology
- New-SPEnterpriseSearchTopology
- New-SPEnterpriseSearchQueryProcessingComponent
- New-SPEnterpriseSearchIndexComponent
- New-SPEnterpriseSearchContentProcessingComponent
- Remove-SPEnterpriseSearchTopology
- Remove-SPEnterpriseSearchComponent
- Set-SPEnterpriseSearchTopology

App Management Service Reference

SharePoint 2013 introduces an "App" paradigm for coded Share-Point solutions along with an online store (or configurable on-premises marketplace). There are several PowerShell cmdlets that may be used when managing Apps in SharePoint.

App Settings and Configuration

Use the cmdlets listed in this section to get or set app configuration settings.

- Get-SPAppAcquisitionSettings
- Get-SPAppAutoProvisionConnection
- Get-SPAppDomain
- Get-SPAppHostingQuotas
- Get-SPAppInstance
- Get-SPAppScaleProfile
- Get-SPAppDisableSettings
- Get-SPAppStateUpdateInterval
- Get-SPAppStateSyncLastRunTime
- Get-SPInternalAppStateSyncLastRunTime
- Get-SPInternalAppStateUpdateInterval
- Set-SPAppAcquisitionSettings
- Set-SPAppAutoProvisionConnection
- Set-SPAppDomain
- Set-SPAppHostingQuotas
- Set-SPAppManagementDeploymentId
- Set-SPAppMarketplaceSettings
- Set-SPAppScaleProfile
- Set-SPAppStateDisableListSync
- Set-SPAppStateUpdateInterval
- Set-SPInternalAppStateUpdateInterval

Denied End Point Management

The App structure in SharePoint 2013 allows you to configure denied end points. Use these PowerShell cmdlets to execute denied end point functions.

- Add-SPAppDeniedEndpoint
- Clear-SPAppDeniedEndpoints
- Get-SPAppDeniedEndpoints
- Remove-SPAppDeniedEndpoint

Installation and Provisioning of Apps

Use the following cmdlets to manage the installation of apps and app packages.

- Disable-SPAppAutoProvision
- Enable-SPAppAutoProvision
- Export-SPAppPackage
- Import-SPAppPackage
- Install-SPApp
- Restart-SPAppInstanceJobs
- Uninstall-SPAppInstance
- Update-SPAppCatalogSettings
- Update-SPAppInstance

Marketplace Management

Use the following cmdlets to manage the marketplace and Office store settings.

- Get-SPAppMarketplaceSettings
- Get-SPMarketplaceConnectionSettings
- Get-SPAppSiteSubscriptionName
- Get-SPOfficeStoreAppsDefaultActivation
- New-SPMarketplaceWebServiceApplicationProxy
- Set-SPMarketplaceConnectionSettings
- Set-SPAppSiteSubscriptionName
- Set-SPOfficeStoreAppsDefaultActivation

Service Application

As far as the App Service Application is concerned, you may only use SharePoint PowerShell to create a new service application or new service application proxy using their respective cmdlets:

- New-SPAppManagementServiceApplication
- New-SPAppManagementServiceApplicationProxy

www.ingramcontent.com/pod-product-compliance
Lightning Source LLC
Chambersburg PA
CBHW071410050326
40689CB00010B/1814